*Lifescripts*

Also by Stephen M. Pollan and Mark Levine

*Live Rich*

*Die Broke*

*Lifescripts: What to Say to Get What You Want in 101 of Life's Toughest Situations*

*Surviving the Squeeze*

*The Total Negotiator*

*The Big Fix-Up: Renovating Your Home Without Losing Your Shirt*

*The Business of Living*

*Your Recession Handbook: How to Thrive and Profit During Hard Times*

*The Field Guide to Starting a Business*

*The Field Guide to Home Buying in America*

# Lifescripts

## *for the Self-Employed*

**Introduction by Stephen M. Pollan**

*Written by:*

Mark Levine, Michael Caplan, Jonathon Epps,
Andrew Frothingham, Erik Kolbell, Deirdre Martin,
William Martin, Nick Morrow, Allison Noel,
Aldo Pascarella, and Roni Beth Tower

Macmillan • USA

Macmillan General Reference
A Pearson Education Macmillan Company
1633 Broadway
New York, NY 10019-6785

Book design by Nick Anderson

Library of Congress Cataloging-in-Publication Data

Lifescripts for the self-employed / introduction by Stephen M. Pollan; written by
Mark Levine . . . [et al.].
    p.    cm.
Includes index.
ISBN 0-02-862621-4
    1. Business communication. 2. Interpersonal communication.
3. Self-employed.  I. Pollan, Stephen M.  II. Levine, Mark, 1958–

HF5718.L523  1999
658.4'5—dc21                                                          98-52419
                                                                          CIP

Manufactured in the United States of America

10  9 8 7 6 5 4 3 2 1

## PART THREE: LIFESCRIPTS FOR PROFESSIONALS, SUPPLIERS, AND OTHERS

I'm the first to admit I don't know everything. I'm always turning to others to fill gaps in my own expertise. So when I was asked to put together this follow-up to *Lifescripts* I knew that to dig deeper into the world of workplace communications and come back with original, creative, and pragmatic new material, I'd need help. In response, I was lucky enough to be able to put together a team of outstanding lifescript authors, each with his or her own unique qualifications, expertise, and approach.

**Mark Levine** is a writer and editor who has collaborated with Stephen Pollan on fourteen books, including the original *Lifescripts* and their recent best-selling contrarian looks at spending and earning money, *Die Broke* (HarperCollins, 1997) and *Live Rich* (HarperCollins, 1998). His work has also appeared in a variety of publications including *Worth*, *New York*, *Money*, and *Working Woman*. He has taught magazine writing at Cornell University, lectured at the Newhouse School at Syracuse University, and his articles have twice been nominated for National Magazine Awards. He lives in Ithaca, New York.

**Michael Caplan** is a freelance writer who lives in New York City. He is currently working in script development with Borracho Pictures.

**Jonathon Epps** is a sales and marketing consultant. He is the owner of The Selling Source, Inc., a consulting firm specializing in architectural specification sales and marketing and professional development. He lives in Ithaca, New York, with his wife, JoAnn Cornish-Epps, and their two children, Paula and Sam.

**Andrew Frothingham** is a Manhattan-based consultant and freelance writer specializing in business communications, including speeches, newsletters, training films, and inspirational T-shirts. He has written, co-written, and ghost-written numerous reference and humor books, including *How to*

*Make Use of a Useless Degree*. He became a full-time writer after careers as a teacher, researcher, advertising executive, and high-tech marketer. He earned two degrees from Harvard, and is now in the process of being reeducated by his young son.

**Erik Kolbell** is a graduate of Brown University, Yale Divinity School, and the University of Michigan. An ordained Congregational minister, Kolbell has served in university and church settings. He is also a licensed psychotherapist practicing in New York City. He has written articles for numerous publications including *Newsweek, The New York Times, Parents,* and *Child.*

**Deirdre Martin** is a full-time freelance writer and member of both the American Society of Journalists and Authors and the Writer's Guild of America. Her work has appeared in a wide variety of publications, including *New Woman, McCall's, Seventeen, YM, Fitness, Bride's, Modern Maturity,* and *InsideSports.* She is the author of *The Real Life Guide to Investing for Retirement* (Avon, 1998) and has written for the daytime drama *One Life to Live.*

**William Martin** spent more than three decades as a high school teacher and associate principal having dialogues with students, teachers, administrators, building staff, and parents. He is now a freelance writer and educational consultant. He lives with his wife, Barbara, in Northport, New York.

**Nick Morrow** is a tax accountant practicing with Martin Geller, CPA, in New York City, and specializes in advising individual and small business clients on a range of tax issues, as well as personal and business matters. He has written articles for numerous publications and lectured before a wide variety of professional organizations. He was a contributing author to *How to Beat the System* (Rodale, 1997).

**Allison Noel** is a freelance writer who specializes in parent-child communications. She is now applying that expertise personally for the first time. She lives with her husband, Jay, in Salem, Massachusetts.

**Aldo Pascarella** is an award-winning screenwriter, with film projects in development at SABAN Entertainment and Brad Krevoy's newly formed production company. A graduate of Dartmouth College and the University of Southern California's Cinema-Television School, he lives in New York City.

**Roni Beth Tower**, a clinical psychologist with a doctorate from Yale University, specializes in issues of work and relationships. A fellow of the Academy of Clinical Psychology and past president of the American Association for the Study of Mental Imagery, she counsels adolescents, adults, and couples at her Westport, Connecticut, practice.

# The Magic of Lifescripts

I've been giving advice to people for most of my adult life. Usually it's in my capacity as an attorney and financial advisor; but other times it's as a son, husband, father, or friend. Most often I'm being asked for help with vital legal and financial matters, but sometimes I'm asked how to persuade a husband to lose weight or how to borrow money from a parent.

I suppose I've become a source of advice on these diverse areas because of my long and varied experience in the law and business, my reputation as an effective negotiator, my notoriety as an author and television commentator, and the uniquely personal brand of service and attention I offer clients, readers, and viewers.

I like to take people by the hand and lead them through a process, helping them plan and preparing them for potential obstacles. I try to break every project down into manageable steps. But despite my best efforts and explaining and coaching there's always one last question: "But what do I *say?*" It doesn't matter if I'm helping a young couple buy their first home, an experienced corporate executive negotiate an employment contract, or my father complain to his insurance company. People always want to know what words they should use and how they should deal with possible responses.

To ease their anxiety, I tell the person to telephone me before the event so we can create a "lifescript" for the whole conversation: an outline of the entire conversation including counters, responses, and rejoinders. Generally the lifescript is used verbatim, but sometimes it simply serves as the extra measure of confidence the person needs to face a difficult, unpleasant, or awkward situation. Many of my clients are amazed at how effective these lifescripts can be, and how much better they fare using them.

I'd like to take total credit for the incredible efficacy of my lifescripts, but while my negotiating savvy and experiences do play a part, what really makes them work is that they're comprehensive plans for situations we usually don't plan for.

When Generals Powell and Schwarzkoff were ordered to attack the Iraqi forces occupying Kuwait they didn't just wing it. They and their staffs sat down and planned for every eventuality. By the time they launched Operation Desert Storm there was nothing that could surprise them. From the first moment to the last they were in charge, dictating the action. They were proactive, not reactive. Saddam Hussein and the Republican Guards didn't know what hit them.

Don't get me wrong. I'm not implying that life is a war—though we all have to deal with our share of petty tyrants and despots. What I'm saying is that if we plan out our interpersonal exchanges—whether they involve work, business, or our family lives—not only will they be easier to deal with but, more often than not, they'll turn out the way we want. With a lifescript, either directly in front of you or just in your head, you'll never be surprised. You'll have a plan that leads inexorably to your goal, regardless of what obstacle is thrown in your way. You'll have an answer to every question, a comeback to every crack, and a defense for every attack.

## HOW TO USE LIFESCRIPTS

The following pages offer solutions for what are arguably 38 of the most perplexing and problematic dialogues a self-employed person will ever face.

Each lifescript begins with a general discussion of the overall *strategy* you should use in the dialogue, usually highlighting what your goal should be. Then the text briefly describes the *attitude* you should adopt—for example, righteous indignation or contrition. The entry then touches on what kinds of *preparation* you need before using the script—perhaps some research or the drafting of a memo. Next, are tips on *timing*—whether it's better to have this conversation on Monday morning or Friday afternoon, for instance. Then the text explains what your *behavior* should be like. This could involve body language or where you hold the conversation.

On the next page is the lifescript itself in flow-chart form. Most offer icebreakers, pitches, possible responses, counters, and retorts. Obviously, each lifescript is different because each conversation takes a different form.

After the flow chart some ideas for *adaptations* are offered—other situations where, with some minor modifications, you could use the same lifescript. Finally, a few *key points* for each lifescript are listed. You can use these as crib notes to bring with you to the dialogue.

These lifescripts can be used verbatim. The words have been chosen very carefully. However, I think it's best if you take the words offered and play around with them until they sound like your own. That's because everyone has different diction and sentence structure. There's nothing wrong with sounding prepared—as long as you sound like yourself.

With 38 scripts and possible adaptations more than doubling that number, I think this book offers help in nearly every common business situation.

However, I'm sure there are important situations I've left out either because the authors and I simply didn't think of them, or because they're unique to you and the circumstances of your life.

Rather than require you to call me on the telephone to help you prepare a personal script, I thought I'd give you a brief course in the five rules behind these lifescripts. That way you'll be able to draft your own. (Though of course, you are welcome to call me if you get in a real pickle.) These are, in fact, the same rules the authors of these lifescripts followed.

## Rule #1: Take Control of the Situation

If you gain nothing else from this book, let it be an understanding of this rule. The single most important element in getting these conversations to turn out the way you want is to take control of them. That doesn't mean you monopolize the conversation or bully the other person. It simply means that, through your choice of words and reactions, you frame and steer it in the direction you want it to go.

In many cases that means you make the first move, and by so doing, force the other person to respond. In other situations, it means responding in such a way that the other person is forced into retorts that you've already prepared to address. Unlike most *icebreakers*, these aren't written just to make the person delivering them more comfortable. They're written to force the other party into a position with a limited number of options. That way we can prepare responses to each of those limited options.

## Rule #2: Say What You Want

I'm continually amazed at the inability of most people to come out and say exactly what they want. Whether it's because we don't want to be viewed as demanding or we're afraid of being turned down, most of us beat around the bush, imply, and drop hints, rather than coming right out and saying what's on our minds.

In almost every lifescript there's a *pitch*: a direct, specific request. You can't rely on other people to infer what you're after or to pick up on your hints. And besides, if you don't come right out and ask directly, you're giving the other party a chance to sidestep the whole issue. Make them respond directly. It's easier to deal with an outright rejection than you might imagine.

## Rule #3: Show Your Power Before You Use It

Subtle demonstrations of power are often just as effective as the outright use of that power. For instance, if you're a restaurant patron you have two powers: your ability to make a scene and your willingness to pay your bill. By calling over a waiter or maître d' and whispering that you're unhappy with your meal and would like another, you demonstrate that you're aware of your power to make a scene, but are holding it in check until they've had a chance to respond. If you actually raise your voice and make a scene immediately you have far less power since you've used up all your ammunition.

Other ways of displaying your power include saying things like, "I'm a longtime customer and would like to continue our relationship," or "The last thing I want to do is hire someone else to finish this project." In both cases you're showing an awareness of your power but a willingness not to use it. That's far more likely to work than an outright threat. Though if push comes to shove, you may have to make such a threat.

## Rule #4: Absorb or Deflect Anger

That doesn't mean you should get angry, however. Displays of anger are just as self-defeating as gratuitous exercises of power. The actual message you send when you get angry is "I have no real power so all I can do is make noise." Therefore, it is important to hold your temper whenever possible.

Similarly, when you're met with anger, the best response is to disarm the other party either by absorbing or deflecting it. You absorb anger by acknowledging it and refusing to respond in kind. ("I can understand your being angry. I would be too.") You deflect anger by suggesting that it's an odd reaction and must therefore be based on something other than your request. ("I don't understand why you're getting angry at me. Have I done something else to bother you?")

## Rule #5: Have the Last Word

In almost every situation it's to your advantage to have the last word in a dialogue. That means either expressing thanks for getting what you wanted, asking for reconsideration of a rejection, or pushing for another meeting or saying that you'll call back if you couldn't get a definite answer. Having the last word does two things: it ensures you retain the control over the dialogue that you seized when you broke the ice, and it allows you to close the conversation on advantageous terms.

The only exceptions to having the last word are in situations where it's important for you to give the other party a chance to "save face." In effect, by giving other people the last word you're letting them think they're still in control, even though they're not.

## TWO PHILOSOPHICAL THOUGHTS

Before you jump into the lifescripts themselves we need to consider two important philosophical issues: the ethics of scripting conversations in advance, and the question of whether or not to use "white lies" to your advantage.

Some of the people I've helped to develop lifescripts have voiced concerns about the ethics of scripting some dialogues. They feel workplace communication is more "honest" when it's spontaneous. Personally, I don't see anything wrong with preparing for office discussions, even informal ones. In fact, I think it's an excellent idea.

Sure, one of the major reasons people like my lifescripts is that they work. By using them my clients have been able to get what they want out of life. But that's not the only advantage to lifescripts. When you plan out a conversation to this extent you avoid a lot of the ancillary problems of human interaction. By scripting you avoid getting sidetracked into a discussion of why you didn't attend an employee's wedding, or why no one from your department participated in the Labor Day walkathon. Granted, those may be two valid topics for discussion. But they should be topics in and of themselves, not background noise in a dialogue about office gossiping or potential vendor problems. By scripting you ensure that the conversation will stay on track and in the process will avoid falling into argumentative patterns. I think that, far from being unfair or unethical, lifescripts help pave the way for smoother workplace relations and better office communication.

Finally, let's look at the issue of white lies. In a few of the lifescripts you'll notice such lines as, "I've already notified the staff about this," which effectively disarm threats from the other party. The authors are assuming that you're actually going to do what the lifescript says, in this case, speak to the staff before the meeting. Of course, that doesn't mean you have to in order to use the line. That's something you'll have to decide for yourself. But if I can offer one more word of advice in parting, it's this: The most effective lifescripts are truthful.

*Stephen M. Pollan*

# I

*Lifescripts*

*...for Clients*

# Cold Calling a New Client

## STRATEGY

There are few things more frustrating and daunting than making cold calls for new clients or customers. But in many businesses, it's a necessity. First, don't try to sell anything in your initial conversation. You'll increase your success rate by simply pushing for a meeting rather than trying to close a sale. Second, have good retorts to the two most common responses—generally these are a vague "not interested," or a cost objection. Third, don't waste your efforts and push more than twice. That will only lead to anger and will waste both parties' time. It's better to move on to another prospect. Assume that you'll get appointments with, at best, 25 percent of those you call, and you'll only close deals with, at best, 20 percent of those you actually meet. Since sales is therefore a matter of volume, your dialogue is necessarily short.

## TACTICS

- **Attitude:** Be enthusiastic, interested, and optimistic. You have to feel as though you are truly offering them an opportunity, so never apologize for calling.
- **Preparation:** Have a written script prepared prior to making your calls.
- **Timing:** Since you'll be working on volume, you're apt to make these calls whenever you have free time. Consider saving your best prospects for the hours just before office hours begin or just after they end, since people are apt to have more time then to listen to your pitch.
- **Behavior:** Don't be antagonistic or condescending. Try to sound spontaneous, even though you're working from a script. Use the other person's name as often as possible. Ask questions to try to direct the conversation. Keep the dialogue short—save your sales pitch for in-person meetings.

# 1. Cold Calling a New Client

**Icebreaker and pitch:** Good afternoon, Mr. Jackson. This is Seth Sterling from Zenith Transportation here in Topeka. Mr. Jackson, the reason I'm calling you today is to introduce you to our new marketing consulting program, which can dramatically increase the effectiveness of your marketing efforts. Mr. Jackson, are you interested in boosting the effectiveness of your marketing?

**Don't need it:** *I'm really not interested, Seth. We don't need any help with our marketing program right now.*

**Heard that before:** Mr. Jackson, I've heard that before from other people in your industry before I had a chance to explain our program. But after hearing about it they decided to enlist our help. Is first thing Thursday morning good for you?

**Financial objection:** *I'm sorry, Seth, we really can't afford to spend money on outside consulting services right now.*

**Cost not a problem:** Mr. Jackson, if it's a question of cost, that's an issue we usually have no problem overcoming. As a matter of fact, Tekno, Inc., which I believe is up the street from you, had the same initial concern until we had a chance to sit down with them. I wonder if we could get together to talk about it. How about 9 A.M. on Thursday?

**Relents:** *You know what, Seth, that sounds interesting. But Thursdays are no good; we'll be tied up all day with deadlines.*

**Still not interested:** *I'm sorry, Seth, I'm really not interested in your service.*

**Propose another time:** I have an opening on Tuesday at 2:00 P.M. Would that be convenient?

**Give up:** I'm sorry to hear that, Mr. Jackson. If you do need a service like ours in the future, please don't hesitate to call us. Thank you for your time, and have a good day.

## ADAPTATIONS

This script can be modified to:
- Request charitable donations
- Solicit political support

## KEY POINTS

- Be friendly, caring, enthusiastic, and above all, concise.
- In response to general objections, say that others said the same thing until they heard about the product or service.
- In response to cost objections, say that's not an insurmountable problem—implying that fees are negotiable—and cite another organization that was able to overcome price objections.
- If you're turned down twice, give up and move on to another prospect.

# Breaking Bad News to a Client

## STRATEGY

Being the bearer of bad news is never easy. It's even harder if you're being paid by the other party, and the bad news directly or indirectly reflects on your abilities. But potential disaster can be averted. The actual language you use depends on who is to blame for the problem. (If you truly are to blame, see Lifescripts 7 and 8, which deal with apologizing to a client for your own or another's mistake.) Remember, however, that in the final analysis you are responsible for your client's problems whether or not you were culpable. That's why it's essential to express your regret and take responsibility, even if there was absolutely nothing you could have done about the situation. From your first words, paint the situation as an obstacle that can be overcome rather than as a disaster, and the sin as one of omission rather than commission. Then, offer your head, or a third party's head, on a platter to your client, along with your plan of action in the hope that your mea culpa and solution will be enough. If it was the client's own fault you should refrain from pointing that out to her directly, and just imply that was the problem. You goal is to explain the situation, offer a solution, and keep the client.

## TACTICS

- **Attitude:** Be apologetic and contrite, but don't grovel or beg for forgiveness.
- **Preparation:** Make sure you know all the facts and can relay them concisely, and have a plan of action that requires only client approval to be set into motion.
- **Timing:** For your own sake the news must come from you, so have the conversation as soon as possible.
- **Behavior:** Holding this dialogue over the telephone implies urgency and also protects you somewhat from anger. Put emotions in personal rather than business terms. Let the client vent—interrupting will only increase her anger.

# 2. Breaking Bad News to a Client

**Icebreaker:** I need to speak with you about an unusual situation that has come up. We've hit a roadblock, but together, I think we can overcome it.

**Third party's fault:** I'm afraid Acme Production has let us down. I just got off the phone with them and they told me they're not going to be able to deliver the spot on time. I've never had a problem with them before; in fact, they were my best vendor. That's why I had chosen them to work on your project. I feel just awful. I've found another production house, Zenith Studios, who can take on the job, and who will absolutely guarantee delivery by the end of next week. I hold myself responsible. What upsets me most is that I've let a friend down. I'm terribly sorry.

**Accepting:** It's not your fault. You can't control your vendors. Just make sure we get the project back on schedule.

**Client's own fault:** I'm afraid the television spot we farmed out to Acme Production isn't going to be completed on time, at least not without a big cost overrun. What's done is done. I was worried about all those special effects we asked for. I had a feeling they couldn't deliver them for the price they quoted. There's no point in assigning blame or fault. But what's important is that we move on from here, learn from the mistake, and make sure we work together even more closely in the future. I suggest we speak with Zenith Studios about taking over the project.

**Angry:** Sorry won't cut it. You might not be to blame but you're responsible. I'm out time and money and your feeling bad won't make those losses go away.

**Accepting:** Don't be ridiculous. How could you plan for a fire? There's no reason to blame yourself.

**No one's fault:** I'm afraid the television spot isn't going to come in on time. I just got off the phone with Acme Production and they told me their facility was destroyed by a fire over the weekend. They saved the preliminary tapes but there's no way they can keep to schedule. I've spoken with Zenith Studios and they're willing to take over the project, but I feel just terrible about this. You're the last person I'd want to let down this way. I keep asking myself, could I have done something, should I have planned for such a disaster?

**Angry:** I don't know if you should have thought about the back-up tapes or not. All I know is my spot is going to be late and I'm out big bucks.

**Reiterate:** I appreciate your understanding. It will never happen again. If you agree, I'll call Zenith and give them their marching orders.

**Deflect:** You're right. I accept full responsibility. From now on I'll come to you for help in selecting outside vendors. Shall I call Zenith and give them the go–ahead?

**Reiterate:** I agree. I'm looking forward to working even more closely with you in the future. For instance, do you agree we should ask Zenith to take on the project?

**Accepting:** *You're right. Blame and fault aren't important. What's important is getting the project back on track.*

**Reiterate:** I appreciate your saying that. You know how important you are to me. If you agree, I'll speak to Zenith right away and get them started.

**Angry:** *You're right. I don't care about who you think is to blame. All I care about is that I'm out time and money.*

**Deflect:** I'm just as upset as you are. But I don't think there's anything to be gained by cursing the heavens. If you agree, I'll contact Zenith and get them started.

**Deflect:** I understand. In the future if anyone, even you, are threatening to throw us off schedule, I'll battle them.

**Asks for concession:** *You do that. Just be aware that I don't want to pay for this fiasco. I expect you to pick up the extra costs.*

**Noncommittal acceptance:** Of course I'll absorb the costs arising from my own mistakes.

## ADAPTATIONS

This script can be modified to:

- Revise the terms of an agreement due to unanticipated events out of your control

## KEY POINTS

- Use words like *obstacle* or *hurdle* rather than *problem* or *disaster.*
- If it's clearly no one's fault, ask if it was your fault.
- If it's a third party's fault, say so, accept responsibility, and offer a plan.
- If it's the client's own fault, say that you need to work more closely in the future, and offer a plan.
- If she gets angry, deflect the anger by saying you understand the response, but urge moving on.
- If she accepts the situation, reiterate your plan.

# Refusing a Client's Request

## STRATEGY

The business world has its share of unethical members. Sometimes you may be unfortunate enough to have one of them as a client. Or perhaps you have a client who wants to use you to do something unethical in order to shield him. In either case, if you don't want or need to keep the client you can simply refuse and tell him to find another professional. But if you need to retain the client, you face a dilemma. The solution is to offer an alternative, ethical course of action that, while it may not lead to the same results, will achieve some of the results without the potential side effects.

## TACTICS

- **Attitude:** You are not a judge and jury, nor a board of ethics. You are simply trying to keep your client from harming himself—and you as well.
- **Preparation:** Understand, and be prepared to discuss, the ramifications of the proposed actions. At the same time, have the groundwork in place for an alternative course. Even if you have completed the alternate planning, don't say so. You want the client to have time to think over what you're saying in this dialogue, and maybe become involved in the planning.
- **Timing:** Do this only after making sure that the request is indeed unethical or clearly improper. Once you've convinced yourself of that, have the dialogue as soon as possible.
- **Behavior:** This dialogue can be done either over the telephone or in person. But in either case, refrain from being condescending and accusatory. Be specific, perhaps alluding to similar experiences you have had.

# 3. Refusing a Client's Request

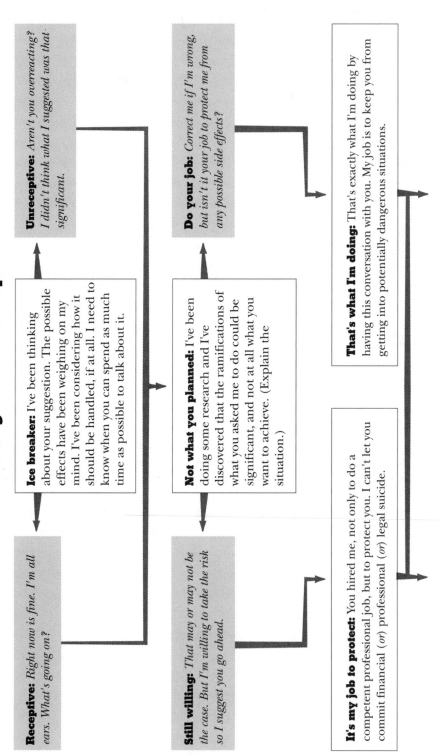

**Receptive:** *Right now is fine. I'm all ears. What's going on?*

**Ice breaker:** I've been thinking about your suggestion. The possible effects have been weighing on my mind. I've been considering how it should be handled, if at all. I need to know when you can spend as much time as possible to talk about it.

**Unreceptive:** *Aren't you overreacting? I didn't think what I suggested was that significant.*

**Still willing:** *That may or may not be the case. But I'm willing to take the risk so I suggest you go ahead.*

**Not what you planned:** I've been doing some research and I've discovered that the ramifications of what you asked me to do could be significant, and not at all what you want to achieve. (Explain the situation.)

**Do your job:** *Correct me if I'm wrong, but isn't it your job to protect me from any possible side effects?*

**It's my job to protect:** You hired me, not only to do a competent professional job, but to protect you. I can't let you commit financial (*or*) professional (*or*) legal suicide.

**That's what I'm doing:** That's exactly what I'm doing by having this conversation with you. My job is to keep you from getting into potentially dangerous situations.

**I'm in charge:** *Listen. You work for me. I've made my own judgment of the risk and I want you to move ahead.*

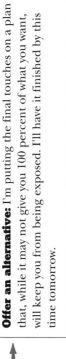

**Refuse to assist suicide:** I'm sorry. I won't help you do something I know will be self-destructive.

**Now receptive:** *All right. Show me how I can get what I want and still stay out of trouble.*

**Offer an alternative:** I'm putting the final touches on a plan that, while it may not give you 100 percent of what you want, will keep you from being exposed. I'll have it finished by this time tomorrow.

## ADAPTATIONS

This script can be modified to:

- Dissuade a family member, friend, or coworker who wants your help in committing some questionable act

## KEY POINTS

- Be professional, not condescending or accusatory.
- Explain the potential ramifications of the proposed action.
- If he is still willing to go ahead, say it's your job to stop him.
- If he insists you just do your job, say that's exactly what you're doing.
- If he demands compliance, say you can't and won't assist in his suicide.
- Close by suggesting another course of action.

# Resurrecting a Former Client

## STRATEGY

Too many businesspeople stand on ceremony and foolish pride and never try to resurrect former clients. That's a mistake. It's far easier to get back together with a client you've lost or had no contact with than to get a new client—just take a look at Lifescript 1. Your goal in this script should be limited: to get a meeting with the former client at which you can pitch to become part of her life once again. The secret to achieving this is to play, as much as possible, on any personal relationship or event the two of you shared. Assuming there was a problem that caused your falling out, the former client may still be angry. Your response should be to absorb her anger and simply ask for the chance to tell your side of the story and to make amends. To do either of those, you'll need to have a meeting.

## TACTICS

- **Attitude:** Be cordial, humble, and, if necessary, persistent.
- **Preparation:** Prior to the call, gather as much personal data about the former client and her family as you can, if you don't remember names and ages. Be prepared to call back since your sudden reappearance may put her off balance initially.
- **Timing:** Try to call either early (before 9 A.M.) or late (after 5 P.M.) in the workday. That way she, rather than her assistant or secretary, is more apt to pick up the telephone.
- **Behavior:** Don't call the former client at home or on the weekend. You'll get the most civil responses when she is at the office. Be prepared to absorb residual anger. If possible, imply that your request is a modest one.

# 4. Resurrecting a Former Client

**Icebreaker:** How are you? I ran into our mutual friend Nancy Jackson yesterday and it got me thinking about you. I'm just calling to patch things up and see how you and your family are doing. I hope I'm not calling at a time when you can't be bothered with a call like this.

**It's a good time:** *Uh . . . no, it's not a bother at all. We're all doing fine. How are you?*

**Miss relationship:** I'm okay. But I think about you often. Even though we no longer have a business relationship, I've always wanted to call and chat and see how you're doing.

**Over anger:** *Listen. I'm over the problem we had. I know you did your best. It just wasn't good enough.*

**Make amends:** That's another reason for this call. I'd like to make amends and work for you again. What happened could never happen again, I think I could really be of help.

**It's a bad time:** *Actually, it is a bad time. I'm very busy at the moment.*

**Say you'll call back:** Oh, I'm terribly sorry. I'll give you a call back later this week.

**Still angry:** *I think about you too . . . every time I look at that boarded-up storefront and the bills I still have to pay.*

**Absorb anger:** I understand your anger. I hope one day you'll be able to sit down with me over a cup of coffee and hear my side of the story. I'm sorry for troubling you.

**Not open to possibility:** *I'm sorry, but you can't turn the clock back. I'm not interested.*

**Open to possibility:** *Hey, I don't harbor grudges. I'd be happy to speak with you.*

**Meet for coffee:** Why don't we just meet for a cup of coffee then? I miss our personal relationship and would really like to see you again—it meant a lot to me.

**Ask for meeting:** I'd like to come down and show you what I've been doing and how it might help your business. I'd really like to resume our friendship—it meant a lot to me.

## ADAPTATIONS

This script can be modified to:
- Rekindle a dormant relationship for networking purposes
- Tell a former customer about a new product or service you're offering

## KEY POINTS

- Be contrite, humble, and personable—this is initially a personal call.
- Explain that you miss the relationship and would like to renew it.
- If she is still angry, absorb the anger and imply that your request is too modest to justify such anger.
- If she is no longer angry but hasn't forgotten the matter, ask for a chance to make amends.
- If she isn't open to renewing the relationship, push for a personal meeting over coffee.
- If she appears willing to renew the relationship, ask for a more formal meeting.

# Dealing with an Irate Client

5.

## STRATEGY

Whether or not you actually made a mistake, an irate client is a problem. If you want to keep the client, you'll want to acknowledge the client's anger quickly, regardless of who's actually at fault, and move forward to finding a solution that will satisfy the client. This is, of course, easier to do if you've had some warning that the client was mad, and have had time to craft a suggested course of action and initiate the dreaded conversation. If a client's anger catches you by surprise, don't hesitate to buy yourself a little time— only a little—by saying you'll look into the situation and call him right back. This gives you a chance to initiate the new interaction and take control of it. Above all, don't respond to the client's anger with anger of your own. It's a natural reaction, but it works against your objective of keeping the client.

## TACTICS

- **Attitude:** Empathize with the client. Tell him you understand his anger. Work from the assumption that you will keep working together, and that, together, you and the client can fix the problem and prevent a reoccurrence.
- **Preparation:** Learn as much as you can about what happened and why the client is angry. (Money? Embarrassment?) Then sketch out a solution that will benefit both of you.
- **Timing:** Keep your preparation time short—this is a situation where a speedy response is important.
- **Behavior:** Start sympathetically. Be prepared to be a bit submissive if you have to in order to diffuse the client's anger. He may need to blow off a little steam, or have you fawn on him a bit, before you can retake the lead in the situation.

# 5. Dealing with an Irate Client

**Icebreaker:** I understand you're upset that we left the "n" out of the headline in the ad for your turnkey system. You have every right to be angry. It's embarrassing. I have a plan to make up for it, and prevent further problems.

**Accepts first apology:** *This couldn't have come at a worse time. Our sales force will catch a lot of grief at the convention. But I guess mistakes happen. So, what's your plan?*

**Remains angry:** *Darn right it's embarrassing. Our whole year depends on this upcoming convention, and we go into it with an ad that makes us a laughingstock?! I'm trying to juggle customers and competitors—and you stab me in the back like this.*

**Restate apology:** You are the most important client this agency has, and we'll do anything we can to regain your trust. I think there may be a creative solution.

**Offer plan:** I've got a full page on hold in the show daily, and have had the creative department develop an ad that stresses that turkey dinners—like your system—are popular, all-American, and come with lots of extras. And then, after the convention, we're putting in a new ad traffic system that will make sure nothing gets run without your sign-off.

**Still angry:** *Are you crazy? I don't see why I should give you clowns another chance.*

**Ask client to suggest solution:** Our relationship is personally very important to me. Since my apology clearly isn't enough, please tell me what I can do to make you less angry. If I can do it, I will.

**Accepts second apology:** *All right—but it had better be good. What's your plan?*

**Pay for it, financially:** *You want to know what you can do? Don't charge me for the media or creative on the ad you screwed up, and run that replacement ad you were talking about.*

**Pay for it, personally:** *You want to know what you can do? Come to Las Vegas and spend five days in our booth at the show so we can have all the wise guys talk to you.*

**Issues threat:** *There's nothing you can do. The only way for me to save face is to sue the heck out of you and make sure all the trade papers know this was your screw-up.*

**Compromise:** *I can't afford to pick up all those costs. Besides, with the new plan, you will have gotten significantly more media and promotional value than under the original plan. Even so, I would be willing to split the costs 50-50 with you.*

**Compromise:** *Even though you are, unquestionably, our most important client, I can't afford to leave my office unmanaged for that week. But I would be willing to rearrange my schedule and come for the opening day and the next day.*

**Warning:** *If you think punishing me is the best way to forward your business objectives, so be it. But please be careful. The business community and both of our staffs know we are friends, and they might respect generosity more than vengeance.*

## ADAPTATIONS

This script can be modified to:

- Deal with an irate investor, mentor, professor, minister, community leader, or member of an older generation who feels that he or she has a right to expect something of you

## KEY POINTS

- Acknowledge and diffuse his anger as quickly as possible.
- Do not respond with your own anger. Anger is a weak position from which to work.
- Once he accepts an apology, proceed directly to pitching your plan.
- If he remains angry, restate your empathy, making a clear apology.
- If he is still angry, involve him in suggesting a solution.
- If he makes a threat, emphasize that his proposed action makes him look like a person out of control. Few people like to be thought of as irrational.
- If he suggests that you pay in some way, try for a compromise where you take only a share of the suggested cost.

# Challenging a Client's Behavior

## 6

## STRATEGY

In most cases, accepting a client's boorish behavior is just part of being a businessperson. The old maxim is true: the customer is always right. You're not going to be able to change someone over whom you have no leverage. But what if the client's behavior or manner is threatening to derail a project? It's in your interest, and your client's interest, to get her under control. The best way to do that is to throw the blame on a third party and to enlist the client in an effort to sway that third party by playacting. In effect you're asking the client to act a certain way, not because her current behavior is inappropriate, but because this new behavior will get what you both want from a third party.

## TACTICS

- **Attitude:** This is one instance where you'll need to be willing to do a bit of acting. Realize that this isn't dishonesty, it's simply the most expedient way to get to your goal. And if you approach the proposal correctly, you won't be telling a lie—you'll just be putting a spin on the facts.
- **Preparation:** Give some thought to exactly what it is about the client's behavior that is problematic, and then develop a plan that will offset the behavior.
- **Timing:** Do this as soon as you realize that your client's behavior is likely to get in the way of achieving your mutual goals.
- **Behavior:** Hold this meeting alone and in person, if possible. That lends the conspiratorial air to the conversation that will back up your spin. Do all you can to deflect suspicion and absorb anger.

# 6. Challenging a Client's Behavior

**Icebreaker:** I need your help in restrategizing the way we approach this whole negotiation. Our meetings with the bank have been too angry and there's too much face-saving going on. In order for us to put some humility into the meetings I think we're going to have to show them by example, and I'm going to need your help with that.

**Angry:** *Listen. Don't tell me about your problems. I'm paying you to take care of this, so just do your job.*

**Absorb anger:** One of the reasons I love working for you is that you can offer excellent input. In this transaction I need to draw on your interpersonal skills and experience in order to keep it moving forward.

**Realizes implication:** *What are you saying? Are you telling me you don't like the way I'm acting at the meetings?*

**Open to new approach:** *Hey, I just want to get what I need from them. I'll do whatever it takes. What did you have in mind?*

**Offer plan:** At the next meeting let's have them do most of the talking. We also need to make them feel like they're very important to us and that we want to maintain our relationship with them. You can do that much better than I, by the way.

**Deflect suspicion:** No, not at all. You've been acting like yourself. It's the transaction and the bank's people that I have a problem with.

## ADAPTATIONS

This script can be modified to:

- Modify or eliminate aggressive behavior, inappropriate language, or a pompous attitude that is having a negative impact on a third party in an office or social setting

## KEY POINTS

- Blame a third party for the problems and enlist the client as your accomplice in an effort to overcome the difficulty.
- If she realizes that you're actually criticizing her behavior, deflect the suspicion and focus matters on the third party.
- If she gets angry, just absorb the anger and directly ask for help in overcoming the problem.
- If she is open to taking a new approach, offer your plan with a dash of flattery.

# Apologizing to a Client for Your Own Mistake

## 7

## STRATEGY

When you've made a mistake that affects a client, financially or otherwise, you're obligated to apologize, not only from a moral point of view but from a business perspective as well. If you want to keep the client you'll need to come clean and offer a plan for addressing the situation. That said, you'll have to make an individual judgment on how far you're willing to go to keep the client. Remember: words cost you nothing other than pride, so I suggest you go pretty far verbally. On the other hand, lowering your fee probably isn't a good idea since it will cut into any future work you do for the client. A compromise solution is to pick up some, but not all, of the costs of cleaning up the problem you created. How much of the cost you absorb is a matter for negotiation.

## TACTICS

- **Attitude:** Be contrite, honest, and apologetic. But move on to the solution as quickly as possible.
- **Preparation:** Do a thorough postmortem so you can completely yet concisely explain what went wrong and why. Have a solution in hand that requires only the client's approval to get launched.
- **Timing:** Do this as soon as possible after the mistake. You want to make sure the client hears about this from you, not from someone else.
- **Behavior:** Having this conversation over the telephone could show a sense of urgency, and can also insulate you somewhat. Be prepared to absorb some anger. However, don't let unjustified threats go by—they're not called for unless your mistake was malicious or your conduct was unethical.

# 7. Apologizing to a Client for Your Own Mistake

**Icebreaker:** I've made a miscalculation that has created a problem for you. I have what I believe is a solution, but first I need to apologize to you. When I was scheduling your project I failed to take into account that there were two religious holidays that fell during the time I'd set aside for printing. We're not going to be able to meet the schedule I laid out for you.

**Accepting:** *I'm not happy about this, but I admire your candor. I want you to know I expect special help from you. Now what's your plan?*

**Angry:** *I can't believe you could have been so stupid and negligent. What were you thinking? Weren't you paying attention? What's wrong with you?*

**Offer plan:** Thanks for your continued confidence in me. I won't let you down. I suggest we start by contacting another, larger printer I've lined up to find out if he can get the job done in time.

**Offers another chance:** *All right. Everyone can make a mistake. How do you plan on working this out?*

**Outright apology:** My relationship with you is very important to me. I feel horrible about what has happened. All I can do is apologize. I don't expect you just to pass this off, but I'd like a chance to earn your confidence back.

**Still angry:** *I can't afford to give you another chance. Not after the screw-up you just made.*

**Ask what can be done:** Our relationship is important to me. Since an apology won't suffice, what can I do that would make up for this mistake? If I can do it, I will.

**Issues threat:** *You've done quite enough already. There's nothing more you can do for me. The only people that can help me now are (your professional association, the Better Business Bureau, or a consumer protection agency).*

**Lower your fees:** *You want to know what you can do? I'll tell you. You can lower your fees. They're too high, especially considering what just happened.*

**Pick up the costs:** *You want to know what you can do? I'll tell you. You can pick up the costs of this fiasco. That's what you can do.*

**Be careful:** If you think punishing me will help your situation, so be it. But I'd urge you to consider such steps carefully.

**Can't do that:** I'm afraid that would only affect the quality of what I do and that wouldn't help either of us. What if I help to absorb some of the cost of this problem?

**Want to keep client:** I simply can't afford to pick up all the costs, but I would be willing to pick up 50 percent of them.

**Willing to lose client:** I wish I could pick up the costs—I really do. But I simply can't do that. I'm sorry.

## ADAPTATIONS

This script can be modified to:

- Explain a material disappointment or injury, created unintentionally by you, to a family member or friend

## KEY POINTS

- Be direct, frank, and contrite. Offer an explanation but not an excuse.
- If he accepts your apology, immediately describe your plan.
- If he gets angry, offer an outright, humble, and candid apology.
- If he remains angry, ask what else you can do.
- If he issues an unjustified threat, urge him to be cautious.
- If he asks you to lower your fees, suggest absorbing some costs instead.
- If he asks you to pick up the costs, say you'll absorb a share of them.

# Apologizing to a Client for Another Person's Mistake

## STRATEGY

When a client calls to tell you that she is upset with one of your staff members, there's really very little you can do about the situation. Your goal is to keep the anger with the individual from being spread on to you and your company. Whether or not you know about the situation, it's best to act as if this is the first you've heard of it. The best response is simply to allow the client to vent. Don't apologize for someone else—that will allow the anger to be shifted to you. Instead, show personal concern, express your regrets over the whole situation, ask if you can bring the matter to the staff member's attention, and then offer to make amends. In most cases, all the client needed to do was to express her anger. By accepting the anger, without accepting blame or rising to your staffer's defense, you should be able to resolve the situation quickly and painlessly.

## TACTICS

- **Attitude:** Be concerned and regretful, not reflexively defensive or apologetic.
- **Preparation:** You'll have little or no time to prepare for specific situations, so put a continuing policy in place for dealing with such issues.
- **Timing:** You'll have no control over the timing of this dialogue.
- **Behavior:** Moderation is the key. If you're too responsive you'll open yourself up for blame. If you're unresponsive you won't give the client a chance to vent. Listen, show you care, offer to do what you can, and leave it at that.

# 8. Apologizing to a Client for Another Person's Mistake

**Makes complaint:** *I'm very upset with your office. I just found out your paralegal insulted my mother when she came to your office to notarize the wills. You know, my mother isn't well, and her getting upset doesn't help her health. I'm very concerned with the way your staff treated her.*

**Show concern:** First, and most importantly, how is your mother feeling? Is she okay?

**Restates softened complaint:** *She's as well as can be expected. Thank you for asking. I know she's hard of hearing and obstinate at times, but that's no excuse for how she was treated.*

**Offer amends:** Thank you for bringing this to my attention. I feel terrible that you had to make this call. May I mention this to my paralegal to make sure it never happens again to your mother or to anyone else? Meanwhile, if there's any way I can make amends, please let me know.

**Final venting:** *By all means talk to her. There's no way to make up for it; just make sure it doesn't happen again.*

**Issues threat:** *You could pack up my files and send them to my new lawyer. That will ensure this won't happen again.*

**Absorb threat:** That's certainly your right. But I hope you'll give us another chance.

**Fire her:** *You could fire her. That will ensure this won't happen again.*

**Absorb anger:** If it happens a second time, I will.

## ADAPTATIONS

This script can be modified to:
- Derail criticism from someone important to you about someone important to you

## KEY POINTS

- Show concern.
- Don't apologize or rise to a defense.
- Offer to make amends.

# Pressing a Client to Pay the Bill

## 9

## STRATEGY

As businesses work to hold on to money for as long as they can, pressing a client for payment is a challenge you're likely to face more and more often. Fortunately, this task is rarely as awkward as you imagine it might be; frequently there has been just a clerical mistake, or the client will at least pretend that there has been one. This often means you will have to let the client look into—or pretend to look into—the matter and schedule a second call. The attitude to take in the first call is that, since you are, in effect, partners, the client's failure to pay promptly is probably an oversight that can be swiftly corrected. In the second call, you should push for performance. Do not let the situation become confrontational unless the client signals a complete unwillingness to pay and you are willing to jeopardize your relationship with the client.

## TACTICS

- **Attitude:** You have performed a service and delivered a product, and it is only reasonable that you be paid promptly. You value this client, and you know he values your services in return. By checking on payment, you are merely following normal business practices.
- **Preparation:** Have the invoices in question in front of you. Know the total amount due, and your client's payment history, including any advanced payments. Also, have all the particulars of the job or jobs in question in front of you: the day the project started, the day of delivery, any positive response it received, any problems or delays that occurred, and any special agreements that were made about payment terms.
- **Timing:** Call during business hours, so the client does not have the excuse that accounting personnel are not available. Call the day after you expected payment.
- **Behavior:** Have this conversation over the phone, so it's less confrontational—but be ready to ask when you can come over and get a check in person. This will emphasize your sense of urgency. Keep things on a business-to-business level. Let the client know the call is standard procedure, not personal.

# 9. Pressing a Client to Pay the Bill

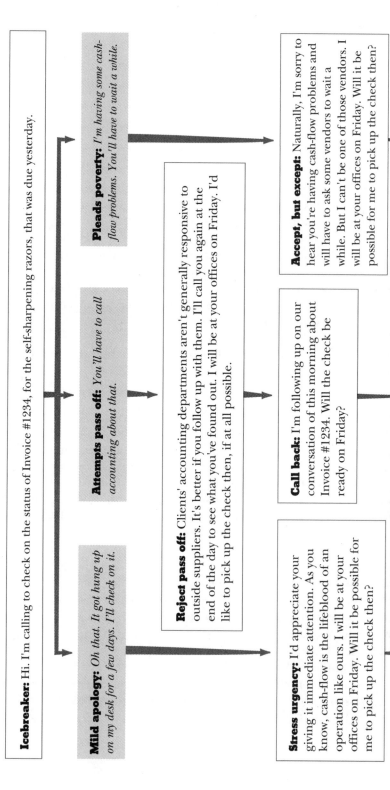

**Icebreaker:** Hi. I'm calling to check on the status of Invoice #1234, for the self-sharpening razors, that was due yesterday.

**Mild apology:** *Oh that. It got hung up on my desk for a few days. I'll check on it.*

**Attempts pass off:** *You'll have to call accounting about that.*

**Pleads poverty:** *I'm having some cash-flow problems. You'll have to wait a while.*

**Reject pass off:** Clients' accounting departments aren't generally responsive to outside suppliers. It's better if you follow up with them. I'll call you again at the end of the day to see what you've found out. I will be at your offices on Friday. I'd like to pick up the check then, if at all possible.

**Call back:** I'm following up on our conversation of this morning about Invoice #1234. Will the check be ready on Friday?

**Stress urgency:** I'd appreciate your giving it immediate attention. As you know, cash-flow is the lifeblood of an operation like ours. I will be at your offices on Friday. Will it be possible for me to pick up the check then?

**Accept, but except:** Naturally, I'm sorry to hear you're having cash-flow problems and will have to ask some vendors to wait a while. But I can't be one of those vendors. I will be at your offices on Friday. Will it be possible for me to pick up the check then?

**Pleads policy:** *I checked with Accounting. Our new company policy is to require three approvals and to hold on to everything for 120 days.*

**Cite implied contract:** I understand that some companies are going that direction, and I can adjust my future pricing to reflect the change. But those aren't the terms under which we have been doing business, or under which we agreed to this project.

**Agrees:** *Okay, I'll send it over today. By the way, are you guys hiring?*

**Won't commit:** *No. I can't even do that.*

**Agrees to pay:** *I found a way to get a check cut on Thursday. I'll see you Friday—but come by early. I have a two o'clock tee time.*

**Express thanks:** I really appreciate this. I knew I could count on your help.

**Negotiate partial payment:** I need to get at least some payment from you so I can avoid turning the account over to Collection. Is there some way to pay this out of discretionary funds? Can you at least pay us half now, and the rest later?

**Negotiate definite date:** It's not going to do either of us any good if I have to turn the account over to Collection. I can stall for two weeks if you fax me a commitment, in writing, to pay in full within two weeks. Can you do that?

**Still cites policy:** *There's no point in that. The bean counters are in control, and I can't get them to budge.*

**Again pleads poverty:** *You don't understand. We are in a real crunch. We may be fine in a while, but right now, no one gets paid a cent.*

## ADAPTATIONS

This script can be modified to:
- Press for alimony or child support
- Collect on a charitable pledge
- Collect condo or co-op dues

## KEY POINTS

- Reject pass-offs. You have no real leverage or relationship with his accounting department, and they are paid to maximize cash flow. Your agreement is with your client contact, and it's his job to get you paid. Resist the suggestion that he doesn't have the power to do so.
- Present this as a shared problem. If you or your client is at a big company, refer to accounting as "them," and you and your client as "us." Otherwise, refer to your accountants or lawyers (other than yourself) as "them."
- Sympathize with him, but press your demands.
- Do not get drawn into a discussion of his situation.

# Telling a Client You've Increased Your Fees

# 10.

## STRATEGY

Increasing your fees is one of the easiest ways to increase your income. But doing so means you'll need to tell your existing clients that their bills will be going up. The best approach is to stress that the increase is absolutely necessary for you to keep giving the client the level of professional service and attention she demands and has come to expect from you. You'll be surprised how many of your clients acquiesce.

## TACTICS

- **Attitude:** This is an announcement, not a request. Don't treat it as a major event: raising fees periodically is part of the normal course of business; all professionals do it.
- **Preparation:** Determine how long it has been since you last raised your fees and what services or capabilities you've added in the interim. Learn whether the client has recently increased her own fees or prices, or if any of the other professionals servicing the client have increased fees. Know where your fees stand relative to your competitors, and have documentation. Be able to cite any increases in productivity or profitability you've helped the client attain. Finally, review your contract to see if it contains any specific procedures for raising rates.
- **Timing:** It's best to have this conversation shortly after the client has had a business success to which you contributed. But don't wait for that to happen. You need to get your higher fee accepted before your next budgeting and planning cycle.
- **Behavior:** Have this conversation face-to-face during regular business hours. Don't wear your Armani suit or your Rolex that day. Take charge of the conversation. It's your job to get this increase; no one else is going to do it for you. Stop the moment you have agreement and go on to other business.

# 10. Telling a Client You've Increased Your Fees

**Icebreaker:** For the past year I've been paying so much attention to my clients' needs, including your own, that I haven't paid enough attention to my own business.

**Pitch:** I met with my accountant and she has shown me that I need to raise my fees so I can still serve you profitably. So, starting next month, my hourly rate will be $100. I think you'll agree that's fair and reflects the value I deliver to you.

**Out of line:** *Look, we'd all like to make more, but don't you think you're making quite enough already?*

**Agree:** *Sure, I understand. Besides, you'll still be getting less than the mechanic who fixes my Jaguar . . . and you're more reliable.*

**Give me a deal:** *I understand why you want to charge new clients a rate like that, if you can get it. But I think you should give us a break. We helped build your business. In a very real way, we paid the tuition for your education in our industry.*

**Fees are gross:** You have to remember my fees are my gross income. I have to take care of all my overhead and expenses from that. When you net it down, I make relatively little, and I don't get paid vacations, sick days, medical coverage, a pension plan, or stock options. When you consider all that, I think it's clear $100 an hour is more than reasonable.

**New fee includes break:** The price I quoted you is one I am offering only to you. I am charging new clients $125 an hour. I quoted you the lower fee because I value our relationship, and I don't want there to be any impediment to our continuing to work together.

**Competitor threat:** *I know you value our relationship. But I also know that if you raise your fees I'll have to choose a new vendor. I got a proposal just last week from another professional who charges only $85 an hour. I've still got it on file.*

**Caution:** That sounds like a bargain—but please think carefully before you do anything like that. Check their references. Some professionals have junior people do a lot of their work. I'm the principal of my operation and I work very hard for you, and I'm very productive. I know your plants, your customers, your sales force, and your intranet system. You'd lose a lot of momentum if you had to bring someone else up that learning curve.

**Still unsure:** *I don't know. I need some time to think.*

**Make appointment:** That's a good idea. Let's make an appointment for three days from now, and in the meantime I'll prepare a more complete presentation about the justification for this increase.

**Express thanks:** Thanks. I enjoy serving you and this increase will let me keep at it.

## ADAPTATIONS

This script can be modified to:
- Tell a business partner that you're increasing your draw
- Tell an investor that you're increasing your salary

## KEY POINTS

- Keep bringing the discussion back to the idea that the increase is reasonable.
- If she compares your fee to a salary, stress that your fee is a gross number.
- If she asks for a special deal, respond that the fee you quoted already represents a special deal.
- If she remains angry, schedule a meeting for a few days later to make a fuller presentation. Do not indicate that there is any room for negotiation.

# Justifying Increased Fees to a Critical Client

## 11

## STRATEGY

Encountering resistance when you tell a client about a fee increase can actually be a good sign—it generally means he wants to keep working with you; now it's just an issue of price. What you need to do is convince the client he is getting a good deal and is actually benefiting by agreeing to your increased fees. Take the position that you and your client are strategic allies, part of a working team, so the client should care about your success as much as you care about his.

## TACTICS

- **Attitude:** This is a business matter. You're doing what you always do—giving your client the background data he needs to make a wise decision.
- **Preparation:** Know how long it has been since you last raised your fees and what services or capabilities you've added in the interim. Know how your profitability has changed during that period. If possible, find out what the normal profit margins are for your profession. Make a list of everything you provide for your client, and note everything you don't charge for that competitors might, such as telephone calls, travel costs, photocopying, and the like. Note any concessions or special breaks you've given the client. Pull any complimentary memos you've received from the client. Be prepared to cite any increases in his productivity or profitability that resulted from your efforts. Know where your fees stand relative to your competitors, and have documentation. Review the client's mission statement and speeches to see if there are any statements about wanting strategic partners to be profitable.
- **Timing:** Give an angry client a couple of days to cool off and use that time to prepare. Consider having this meeting before or after regular business hours to make the point that you're busy attending to his needs during your regular hours.
- **Behavior:** Have the meeting in whatever space you normally use for strategic planning sessions. Remain cool and confident of the logic of your position. Don't get defensive or angry. Don't plead. Above all, don't negotiate.

# 11. Justifying Increased Fees to a Critical Client

**Icebreaker:** I appreciate that you need to understand the context for a fee increase. I'm sure that by the time I've given you all the facts, you'll see that paying me the increased fee is not only fair, it's also a good investment on your part.

**Out of line:** *Cut the sales pitch. I'm disappointed in you. This increase is totally out of line. You know we're cutting costs and have to cut staff, but you're going the other way and asking for more.*

**Unfair to employees:** *All that's irrelevant. The point is I can't give my employees raises right now, so I can't very well give you the increase you asked for.*

**Too big an increase:** *I could sign off on a small increase, but this is too big. Your expenses haven't gone up that much. I don't see how you can justify this.*

**Blames bosses:** *This kind of nonsense could get me into all sorts of trouble with my management. I've already put in for my budget for the year and I'm supposed to trim it 10 percent and it's already down to the bone.*

**For your benefit:** I'm aware of your staff reductions. That's why I need to be sure that I'd be here for you when you need me for some of the functions you're going to outsource. I'm increasing my fees—so my operation will stay healthy and available to you.

**Not an employee:** I'm not an employee. I get none of the benefits or security. You may be controlling your costs, but you're certainly not controlling your income —we're working like crazy together to increase it. My efforts are aimed at contributing to your revenue stream. I think it's appropriate for you to invest a small amount in the continuing vitality of my part of your team.

**Brings me to market value:** I'm charging you the same rate I charged before I got an office, and before I got a cell phone and beeper so you could reach me twenty-four hours a day. I'm charging well below my market value. I've paid closer attention to your business than mine. I will be charging you less than I would a new client. I think that kind of loyalty deserves some support.

**Offer solution:** Not having me on your team would cause a greater shortfall in your budget than paying the increase. I've helped you raise revenues and control costs, and it's a lot less expensive to pay me as a vendor than as an employee. I'd be happy to go over your budget in detail with you and see if I can help you find a way to generate the savings you need to cover my fee.

**Agrees:** *Okay, I'll pay it. But I still think it's steep. At those prices you'd better talk quickly on the telephone, and I'm sure not going to pay for you to attend our sales meeting.*

**Thanks:** I'm glad we have that matter settled because I'm eager to keep my focus on your business needs.

**Competitor threat:** *Haven't you been listening? I said no. Your old fee is what I have in the budget, and that's what I'm willing to pay. Either work for that or I'll find someone else.*

**Leave door open:** I've already worked for you for below market rates and I'm offering you a discount. As much as I want to keep working with you, I can't work for less. It would be unfair to my wife, my children, and myself. But I want you to know that I'll be here if you find that my new rate was a good deal after all.

**Better use of time:** My new fee is at or below the market for the quality and service I deliver. If you go to someone else you may not get the same kind of intense attention from a principal that I give you. I think it would be better to pay me what I'm worth and devote your valuable time to your core business.

**Stays angry:** *I'll tell you what a bad use of time is—this meeting. You know my position: no fee increase. Take it or leave it.*

## ADAPTATIONS

This script can be modified to:
- Renegotiate a contract at renewal

## KEY POINTS

- Focus the discussion on the value you bring him, positioning yourself as a contributor of revenue, not an expense.
- After you answer each objection, push for agreement.
- If he mentions cutbacks, tell him that's why he needs you to remain a viable outside resource.
- If he raises the issue of fairness to his employees, answer that you're not an employee.
- If he objects to the size of your increase, show that you're just bringing your fee up to market level.
- If you're unable to get agreement, leave the door open by showing that there are no hard feelings and indicating your willingness to come back on board—at the new fee.

# Renegotiating Your Fee with a Client

*12.*

## STRATEGY

There are times when your original estimate of how much an assignment will cost turns out to have been wrong. If you're going to end up with less of a profit than you'd like, or you're going to break even, it's best simply to accept the situation as is, and learn from it. However, if you're going to end up losing money it's worth trying to renegotiate your fee. The secret to doing this successfully is demonstrating that the project is more complex than you'd originally thought, and that in order for you to do the quality of work you'd promised you'll need to increase your fee. By admitting you've made a mistake and linking the quality of the job to the increased fee, you may be able to get by with only a minimal amount of anger or annoyance from the client. However, be aware that you're putting your long-term relationship with the client or customer at risk.

## TACTICS

- **Attitude:** Realize that you're going to have to admit an error in judgment and that you'll be placing your long-term relationship at risk.
- **Preparation:** Prior to the conversation, have ready an explanation for your miscalculation and a plan for moving forward. In addition, have an answer ready if the client tries to negotiate the amount of the increase.
- **Timing:** Do this as soon as you realize your original estimate was wrong.
- **Behavior:** You can have this conversation over the telephone. Absorb any anger or resentment, but stress that the quality of service is contingent on an increase in the fee. Indicate that you're only looking to break even. Don't press for a final answer in this conversation.

# 12. Renegotiating Your Fee with a Client

**Icebreaker and pitch:** Cheryl, this is Jane. You're not only one of my most important clients, but you've also become a close friend. That's why I have to share with you a problem I have with the estate plan you asked me to prepare for you. In order for me to do an effective job I've got to bring in a tax expert. Of course, I'm not going to mark up her cost, but it will increase the price another $2,000.

**You said you could do it:** *I thought you were an expert in this field. That's what you told me. If you had told me I needed an expert I would have gone to one in the first place.*

**I can but . . . :** I am an expert. My reputation is important to me and so is the quality of what I do. That's why I'm recommending we get a second opinion. Besides, you couldn't go directly to this kind of expert.

**Eat it:** *You can't make that my responsibility. I relied on your price to get my husband to agree to this project. You're a businesswoman. When I make a mistake I have to eat it. This is your problem, not mine.*

**Quality at risk:** Look, the whole issue here is that I want to do the best job possible for you. I can, if you wish, stick to the original price. But I have to warn you that we're taking a risk. The decision is yours.

**How did this happen?:** *I don't understand how this could happen. A month ago you said the price would be $10,000. Nothing has changed. Why has the price gone up?*

**Not extraordinary:** I understand your confusion. What happened isn't that extraordinary. We've just discovered that you're a wealthier woman than you thought. That means we need to bring in another specialist.

**Forget it:** *I can't afford that. Maybe we should just forget about it and continue another time when I have the money.*

**I've already done work:** That would be extremely difficult for me. I've already invested over 100 hours of my own time in this project.

**Needs time:** *Let me think about it and get back to you.*

**Agree:** Of course. I hope you decide to continue. But in any event I'll prepare a bill for what I've done so far.

**Forget it:** *Let's just forget the whole thing for now.*

**Can't:** That would be hard for me since I've already invested over 100 hours of my own time in the project.

**Split it?:** *What about if we split the additional cost?*

**Try to cut fee:** Let me go back to the specialist and see if I can get her to reduce her fee as a professional courtesy and then I'll eliminate some of my own profits.

**Agrees:** *Okay, but don't come back to me with any more surprises.*

**Reinforce decision:** I think you're doing the right thing. This isn't something we want to take any chances with.

## KEY POINTS

- Stress the importance of the relationship, personally and professionally, as well as the need to provide top quality.
- If she wants to abandon the project, note that you'll need payment for what you've already done.
- If she asks how this could have happened, stress the increased complexity.
- If she asks you to absorb the cost, suggest that that would lead to lower quality.
- If she questions your professionalism, explain that that's exactly why you've spotted the need for additional work.
- If she suggests splitting the added cost, respond with a proposal of your own.
- If she won't pay for completed work, see Lifescript 9: Pressing a Client to Pay the Bill.

# Explaining Delays to a Client

*13.*

## STRATEGY

Delays are a fact of life in business. But explaining them to an anxious client or customer isn't easy. Whether the delay was caused by your own miscalculation about your capacity or by an objective circumstance doesn't matter at this point. Since a delay is now unavoidable, there's nothing to be gained by going into detailed explanations of what went wrong. In any case, the client is probably not interested in why anyway. The secret here is to do whatever you can—short of delivering on time—to accommodate the client. If that means cutting into your profits, so be it. In order to make the delay tolerable you have to offer something on the promised date. While it may not be all the client wants, at least he won't be empty-handed.

## TACTICS

- **Attitude:** Realize that you're going to take some heat for this and risk losing the client.
- **Preparation:** Have ready a very brief and vague explanation of the problem, and prepare a plan that will offer the client something on the promised date of delivery.
- **Timing:** Do this as soon as you realize the scheduled delivery is impossible.
- **Behavior:** Have this dialogue over the telephone—you don't want it going on too long. Absorb any anger and accept full and total responsibility, even while noting that the situation was beyond your control. Then offer your partial product or service and explain how this might be sufficient for the time being. Finally, let the client have the last word—it will help him save face since there's really no alternative but to accept the situation.

# 13. Explaining Delays to a Client

**Icebreaker and pitch:** I'm calling to let you know the brochure will not be ready in time for your sales meeting before the trade show in Las Vegas. We've had a technical problem at the printer. I'll be able to get them to you the morning of the day the trade show opens.

**Fearful:** *How could you do this to me? You know I've got to have that brochure before the show to prep the sales staff.*

**Angry:** *You've had more than enough time to get this done. If I can't count on you for this, I can't count on you for anything.*

**You're responsible:** *How do you plan on dealing with this? What are you going to do?*

**Don't worry:** There's no reason to panic. The delay was beyond my control. I think I have a solution to your problem.

**Anger won't help:** Please don't prejudice our relationship over something that was unavoidable and beyond my control. If you let me, I can tell you my solution to this problem.

**Take responsibility:** The delay is unavoidable and beyond my control but I take full responsibility for it. I think I have a solution, however.

**Offer solution:** I can have working drafts of the brochure, without the edited copy, retouched photos, and four-color graphics, for all your salespeople by the end of the week. That way you'll be able to go over the brochures with them prior to the trade show.

**Takes parting shot:** *Well, I've got no choice, have I, so I suppose that will have to do. But you better come through this time . . . understand?*

## ADAPTATIONS

This script can be modified to:

- Counter any frustrations you expect from a third party who isn't going to receive what he or she anticipated

## KEY POINTS

- Be businesslike, direct, and concise. State explicitly that there will be a delay and that there's no way to avoid it.
- If he expresses fears, explain that panic isn't necessary and offer your plan.
- If he holds you responsible, accept responsibility and offer your plan.
- If he gets angry, absorb the anger and offer your plan.
- Let him have the last word.

# Closing a Deal with a Client

*14.*

## STRATEGY

Most salespeople know that in order to make a sale you actually have to ask for a decision. But by directly asking potential customers, you're putting them on the spot. Some will opt to buy. A few will be equally direct and give you a flat-out no. But most will equivocate or stall, either because they're still unsure, they're afraid to say no, or they need a little bit more convincing. This script differs from most of the others in this book in that, rather than going through a complete dialogue, it concentrates on one part of the conversation, offering a series of responses to particular stalls.

## TACTICS

- **Attitude:** It's better to push beyond a stall and either force a direct no or get more information so you can close more effectively.
- **Preparation:** In this case, preparation is more a matter of memorizing the responses you feel are most appropriate to your business.
- **Timing:** Ask for a decision as soon as you've finished your pitch.
- **Behavior:** Even though the language may seem a bit confrontational, if delivered in a caring, friendly tone it will simply be taken as a sign of persistence and concern.

# 14. Closing a Deal with a Client

I'd like to add your name to our client list. Shall we move ahead and fill out the order form?

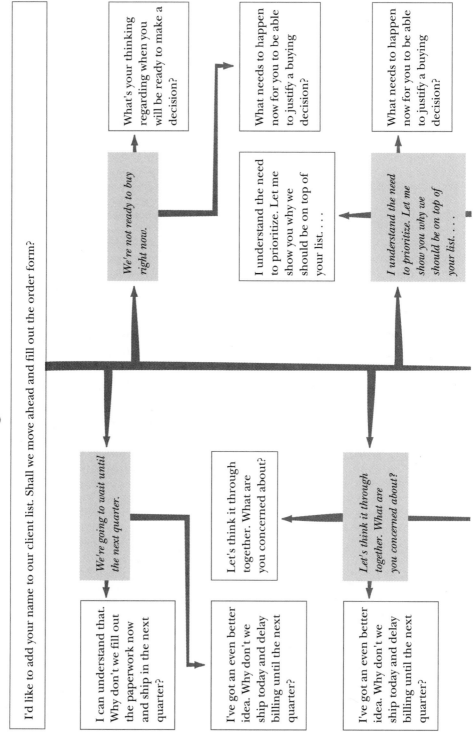

What's your thinking regarding when you will be ready to make a decision?

We're not ready to buy right now.

What needs to happen now for you to be able to justify a buying decision?

I understand the need to prioritize. Let me show you why we should be on top of your list. . . .

I understand the need to prioritize. Let me show you why we should be on top of your list. . . .

What needs to happen now for you to be able to justify a buying decision?

We're going to wait until the next quarter.

I can understand that. Why don't we fill out the paperwork now and ship in the next quarter?

Let's think it through together. What are you concerned about?

I've got an even better idea. Why don't we ship today and delay billing until the next quarter?

Let's think it through together. What are you concerned about?

I've got an even better idea. Why don't we ship today and delay billing until the next quarter?

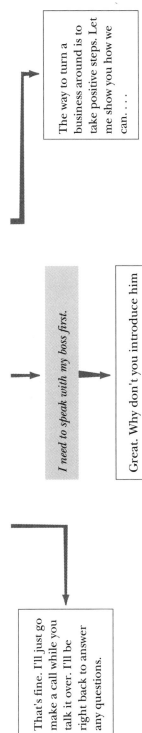

*I need to speak with my boss first.*

Great. Why don't you introduce him to me and let me do the work? That's my job, after all.

The way to turn a business around is to take positive steps. Let me show you how we can. . . .

That's fine. I'll just go make a call while you talk it over. I'll be right back to answer any questions.

## ADAPTATIONS

This script can be modified to:

- Force a client to take an important step that he or she is delaying

## KEY POINTS

- Be caring and friendly and your effort to close won't sound confrontational.
- If the customer asks for more time, try to find out what the time is needed for.
- If the customer implies she'll buy later, push for a commitment now and either delivery or payment in the future.
- If the customer has to get approval, offer to help.
- If the customer isn't ready to buy, find out what would make her ready.
- If the customer cites poor business, either make the offer more affordable or show how it can boost business.

# Ending the Relationship with a Client

*15.*

## STRATEGY

Ending a relationship with a client is always difficult, in part because most of us have been trained to fight tooth and nail to retain clients. At the same time, the client is usually accustomed to thinking he has the upper hand in the relationship and may be surprised when you overtly take control and end things. On top of that, the relationship with a client is often a very close one, and the client could feel personally betrayed. The best strategy in this situation is to make it clear that this is a business decision made in his best interests, as well as yours; it is not a personal decision. You will want to make it clear that this is a final decision, which has already been agreed to by your associates, if you have any.

## TACTICS

- **Attitude:** Realize that this conversation could be awkward for both of you, but the sooner it's done, the better for all.
- **Preparation:** Be sure you and your colleagues are ready to make this move. Assess how it will affect your business and your income. Review your contract to see if there are any procedures you must follow.
- **Timing:** Hold this conversation as soon as you are ready, preferably just after the client has paid your most recent invoice.
- **Behavior:** This conversation is best held over the telephone. Just make sure you call your client at the office, not at his home, reinforcing your position that this is a business, not personal, decision.

# 15. Ending the Relationship with a Client

**Icebreaker:** I've always tried to make sure our relationship was mutually beneficial. We've analyzed the current situation and realized that our companies would both be better served under a different arrangement. Accordingly, we'll be ending the business relationship between our two companies.

**Misinterprets:** *I know we've been paying late. Let me prod the guys in accounting. How about tennis at two this afternoon?*

**Correct:** This isn't about late payments or changing our personal relationship.

**Assigns blame:** *Your wife is still upset about what I said to her! That didn't mean anything. I'll send her some flowers. Come on, we've got work to do.*

**No blame:** This has nothing to do with my wife. It's strictly a business decision.

**Gets angry:** *How dare you suggest that after all I taught you about the business? We've been your key client; I give you great references. Why, I even sponsored your membership at the racquet club and introduced you to my sister Edwina. You owe me. Quit screwing around and think about my business for a change. I'm the client.*

**Stress friendship:** I appreciate all that, and I'm hoping that we'll still be friends. I love the club and have great respect for Edwina's cooking. But this is about what's best for both our businesses.

**Accepts:** *I guess you're right. But it was great while it lasted, wasn't it? Besides, now that I'm no longer your client, maybe you'll be a better competitor on the tennis court.*

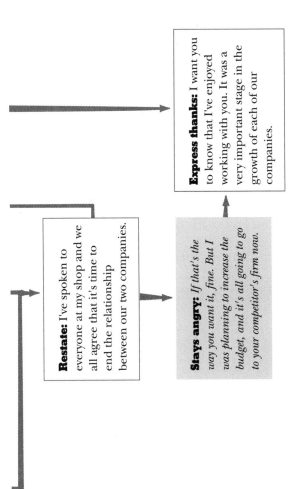

**Restate:** I've spoken to everyone at my shop and we all agree that it's time to end the relationship between our two companies.

**Stays angry:** *If that's the way you want it, fine. But I was planning to increase the budget, and it's all going to go to your competitor's firm now.*

**Express thanks:** I want you to know that I've enjoyed working with you. It was a very important stage in the growth of each of our companies.

## ADAPTATIONS

This script can be modified to:
- Leave a shared workspace
- Leave a shared residence
- Go from being an in-house service to an independent company

## KEY POINTS

- This is final: do not offer any hope for appeal.
- If he misunderstands, restate your decision.
- The decision, not the reason for it, is what matters.
- If he seeks to assign blame, stress that this is a business decision agreed to by all your partners.
- If he gets angry, appeal to your personal relationship and stress that it's a business decision.
- Don't get into a debate. Whether he accepts or stays angry, express thanks and get off the telephone.

# II

# Lifescripts

# ...for Investors and Lenders

# Approaching an Institutional Investor

*16.*

## STRATEGY

Just as with job interviews, getting interviewed by an institutional investor means you're more than halfway to getting what you want, which in this case is money. Since they've already seen your business plan and supporting documentation and have agreed to meet with you, they're interested. They think your idea is a good one. They've tested the validity of your numbers. They've found that your proposal meets their criteria. What they haven't done is evaluate the quality of management—and that's you. This meeting is all about you overcoming any hesitations they may have about your ability to manage a growing company. Everything about you—from your apparel and manners to the words you choose and the way you say them—is under a microscope. Pass this audition and you'll get your money. Beyond that, the secret to responding correctly to their questions is understanding what it is they're looking for . . . and giving it to them.

## TACTICS

- **Attitude:** You can be secure that your plan or application has passed inspection, otherwise you wouldn't have the interview. Now it's just you they're concerned with. Be confident, enthusiastic, eager, and alert.
- **Preparation:** You must know everything there is to know about your business plan, including the life stories of your proposed staff and your ideas for expansion. Learn as much as you can about the investor. Prepare a list of questions of your own to ask them.
- **Timing:** The meeting should be scheduled at their convenience.
- **Behavior:** Dress and act as you would if on a job interview for your dream position with your ideal company. Expect more than one person to be in the room, and respond to each the same way—as if they were the most important person in the world. Never interrupt.

# 16. Approaching an Institutional Investor

**Invite inquiries:** I'm really very pleased to discuss my proposal with you. Investors like you offer my plan its best chance for success. From what I've heard about your company, you could contribute tremendously to my business by providing experience and wisdom. I'd be happy to answer any questions you might have.

**Succession?:** *Tell us about your support people.*

**Not solo operation:** I picked them not only because I've had a great deal of experience with them, but because each is knowledgeable in more than one discipline. I've never had to worry when I've been away on a sales call.

**Open to advice?:** *You have a strong marketing background, but how will you make up for your lack of experience in finance?*

**Validity?:** *How did you arrive at such optimistic numbers?*

**Conservative numbers:** I spent an enormous amount of time in validating my sources of revenue, and I tried to be very conservative. I too was pleased with the results.

**Ready for competition?:** *How do you expect to compete against the big guys when they see your success and copy your product (or) service?*

**Authorship?:** *We think your plan is very interesting. Who helped you write it?*

**My plan:** The plan is essentially mine. Of course I had my lawyer and accountant look at it as well.

**Support at home?:** *To what extent will your family get involved in the business?*

**Committed?:** *You've held down lots of different jobs before this. Can you explain that?*

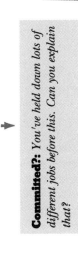

**I'm ambitious:** Each job was better than the last, with more interesting companies, more responsibilities, and higher salaries.

**Looking for exit:** *What's your ultimate goal for the company?*

**Grow and go public:** My ultimate goal is to bring the company public so that it can grow exponentially and become a significant player in this industry.

**Open to guidance:** *How do you feel about a few people from our company being on your board?*

**No problem . . . but:** I have no problem with people operating in an advisory capacity. I'm always seeking out advice and guidance. . . . I do however, need the freedom to manage.

## ADAPTATIONS

This script can be modified to:
- Deal with college or graduate school interviews
- Deal with interviews for political positions

## KEY POINTS

- Be confident, eager, and enthusiastic.
- Questions about authorship are an effort to determine whether you're truly the person behind the idea.
- Questions about your staff are attempts to find out if the business will remain afloat if you leave or die.
- Questions about your numbers are designed to see if you're conversant with finance.
- Questions about your family are probes to see whether they support your efforts.
- Questions about your lack of experience in an area are intended to test your openness to advice.
- Questions about your job-hopping are tests of your commitment and determination.
- Questions about your response to future competition are probes for long-range planning.
- Questions about your ultimate goals are efforts to make sure the investor has an acceptable exit.

# Approaching a Family Investor

*17.*

## STRATEGY

Entrepreneurs can almost never get start-up funds from a bank. Instead, they must turn to family and friends—as well as their own resources—for the money to turn their dream into reality. This is one script where the preparation is more important than the actual dialogue. Your targets must be selected carefully. The one objection you can't overcome is their lack of funds, so make sure they've got the money to possibly help you. You also must have enough solid information for them to make an investment decision. Your business plan— prepared with the help of a CPA—should not only show them when they'll recover their investment, but also project a time when they'll be receiving a yield for their money, and ultimately an exit. Your plan should also be firmly grounded with market projections that show its viability. Even though they're friendly investors, these folk shouldn't feel as though they're getting any less for their money, or taking any greater risks, than they would with any other comparable investment. Your relationship with them should be the reason they choose your business to invest in rather than some other equivalent investment, not a reason to take a risk they wouldn't otherwise take.

## TACTICS

- **Attitude:** Be positive and confident. Any doubts you have will translate into reasons for them to turn you down.
- **Preparation:** Not only should you have a thoroughly documented, professionally prepared business plan for them or their advisors to study, but you should also have selected them carefully. You can't overcome their actual lack of funds.
- **Timing:** Approach friendly investors only after you've got all your plans and projections in place. Going to them too early will mark you as an amateur and your business as just a pipe dream. Schedule the meeting for nonbusiness hours to accentuate your personal relationship.
- **Behavior:** Try to hold this meeting at their home. Suggest that both spouses be present. At the same time, keep your conversation businesslike. Both gambits will accentuate the personal links. The timing and setting should suffice for setting the context. Combine your search for cash with a quest for advice from a potential mentor. That makes the discussion less confrontational. It's a thin disguise, but one that makes both parties more comfortable.

# 17. Approaching a Family Investor

**Icebreaker:** I've come to you for a combination of advice and help. I have some really good news. I've decided to leave my job and go into business. I've been waiting for the right moment, saving money, researching, and studying, and the time has come.

**Happy and open:** *That's great. I'm happy for you. What can I do to help?*

**Thanks:** Thanks so much for being receptive and willing to listen.

**Warning:** *Take it from me. Put your money in the bank and hold on to your job. Business is just a heartache.*

**You see:** What you've just said is why I'm speaking with you. You have a lot of insight about the ways of business.

**Outright negative:** *I'm not the one to help you.*

**You are:** I think you are. Of all the people I know you're the most creative and savvy about business.

**Subtle negative:** *I don't discuss business with family and friends. Why don't you call my office instead?*

**I need you:** I'm seeing you because I need advice. I'd like a hearing. Then I'll give your office a call.

**Pitch:** Over the years I've developed what I've been told is an excellent business plan for (explain idea). I'm prepared to start raising money to supplement my own resources. What I need is your stamp of approval and your financial help. Let me tell you the details. (Present plan.)

**Overly invested:** *Sounds interesting, but I'm overly invested right now.*

**Big gamble:** *Sounds interesting, but these small start-ups are really just crap shoots.*

**Age fear:** *Sounds interesting, but should someone my age put so much in something this risky?*

**Speak to others:** *Sounds interesting. But like I said, you need to speak with my office about these things.*

**Need you first:** I'll be happy to, but I need your reaction and instincts. Take a look at this cash-flow statement.

**Thought of that:** I thought of that. I think this will pay off fairly quickly. Take a look at this cash-flow statement.

**Not this one:** I recognize lots are, but this one isn't. Here, just take a look at the cash-flow statement I've had prepared.

**Make exception:** That may be, but I think when you see this cash-flow statement you'll be willing to make an exception.

**Present cash flow:** Look at these numbers. As you can see . . .

**Just numbers:** *Those are just numbers. How do I know it will work out the way you're planning?*

**Speak to office:** *Looks good. I'll recommend it to my office. You can follow up with them.*

**Speak to other:** *Looks good. But first I need to speak with my accountant.*

**Come back:** *Looks good. Come back to me when you've raised the rest of your money.*

**Being conservative:** I've been very conservative in my planning. Let's sit down with your accountant to verify my figures.

**Meet both:** That's great. I'm eager to meet with you and your staff. I'll call and set up a lunch for all of us.

**Be there:** That's great. I'd like to sit in. I've got some information about how this could be very useful to someone in your tax bracket.

**Need commitment:** Thanks. I just need your commitment, subject to my raising the rest. That makes raising it easier.

**Closer:** I just want to thank you again for your time. I knew you'd be the source of wonderful advice.

## ADAPTATIONS

This script can be modified to:
- Ask relatives for money to pay for a wedding
- Ask relatives for money to pay for college tuition

## KEY POINTS

- Be confident, well prepared, and businesslike. Let your personal relationship speak for itself.
- Whatever the initial response to your statement about going into business, move directly into your pitch.
- Your response to secondary objections should lead directly into presenting your projections of their potential return on investment.
- Qualms about the accuracy of your numbers should be met by a request to meet with the relative's advisor.
- Requests that you speak with his advisor should be met with enthusiasm and a request to have your relative attend the meeting.
- If he begs off, saying he'll speak with his advisors, ask to come along.
- If he doesn't want to be the first investor, ask him to make a verbal commitment subject to others investing too.

# Asking an Institutional Lender for More

*18.*

## STRATEGY

It's surprisingly simple to get an institutional lender to increase the amount of her loan to you, as long as you know which buttons to press, and whom to ask. The key is to approach the loan officer who sponsored your original loan. Part of her job was to make sure the bank was loaning you enough money to generate the kind of revenue required to pay off the loan. She will be anxious to keep you from defaulting and making her look bad. She's concerned, not with your business's long-term health, but with your being able to pay back the money you already owe her. If you can impress on her that you need additional funds to be able to pay her back, you're likely to turn her into a strong ally. And if you can provide her with ammunition to make your (and her) case, it's even better. Hold some information back early in the conversation so you force the banker to ask obvious questions. That will help you steer the conversation where you want it to go.

## TACTICS

- **Attitude:** Be direct and clear. You need help in order to pay off her loan to you in accordance with its terms, not in order to keep your company afloat.
- **Preparation:** Draw up a new loan proposal that offers the bank as much comfort as possible. Include opinions from lawyers and accountants if appropriate.
- **Timing:** Do this as soon as you know you'll have a problem. Bankers hate surprises.
- **Behavior:** Subtly make it clear you know the banker is in this mess with you. Use words like "we" and "us" that reinforce the idea. Stress that there's nowhere else for you to go and without the added funds you won't be able to pay off your loan in the manner promised.

# 18. Asking an Institutional Lender for More

**Icebreaker:** I need to speak to you about a problem we have. The company has had some incredible bad fortune, but I think that, together, we can solve the problem.

**Asks for info:** *What's the problem? What's gone wrong?*

**Offer explanation:** We've had a train-carload of onions go rotten on the siding because the refrigeration in the car failed. The insurance company is refusing to pay, and as a result we're going to have a shortfall in our cash. We're going to be litigating against the insurance company, but that will take some time. We need $100,000 to sustain ourselves while that's going on.

**Asks for risks:** *What's the alternative? What will happen if you don't get the $100,000?*

**Grave . . . but I'll help:** I don't want to even look at that possibility since it probably means a Chapter 11. I've prepared a memo for your lending committee with an opinion from my lawyer. The numbers I've drawn up show how the request fits the bank's lending criteria. I think with this information you'll be able to cover all your bases with the loan committee and make an advance to protect your investment. In addition, if you'd like me to come with you to speak to the committee I'd be happy to.

**Offers thanks:** *Thanks for preparing the memo. That will save me a lot of time and work. I'll let you know when the next meeting of the loan committee will be. Maybe I'll ask you to be there.*

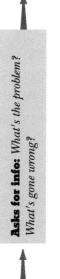

## ADAPTATIONS

This script can be modified to:
- Obtain the return of collateral for use with an alternate lender
- Obtain additional time or inventory from a supplier or creditor

## KEY POINTS

- Be direct, honest, and willing to do all you can to help.
- Make it clear—subtly, if possible—that you know the banker is at risk too.
- Leave information out of your early statements, forcing the anxious banker to ask obvious questions. This will let you control the direction of the conversation.
- If possible, try to demonstrate that you (and the banker) weren't responsible for the situation.

# Asking Institutional Lender to Recast Terms

*19.*

## STRATEGY

Asking an institutional lender to recast the terms of an existing loan can be an uphill battle. Even though the last thing the lender wants is for you to default, he will try to do everything possible to get you to go to another lender to fulfill your obligations to him. Recasting your original loan will require the same kind of approval required for your initial loan. And this time you've acknowledged that your ability to pay back the loan is no longer the same. You need to demonstrate that this inability is due to something totally beyond your control, and that you still have the willingness to pay it back.

## TACTICS

- **Attitude:** Be concerned, but also confident, in the inherent strength of your business, and secure in the knowledge that the last thing the lender wants is for you to default.
- **Preparation:** You must have comprehensive documentation of the problem, as well as the same kind of thorough proposal you used to secure the loan initially, but this time it should demonstrate your ability to pay back the recast loan.
- **Timing:** Do this as soon as you realize you'll have problems. The worst thing you can do is surprise a banker by not making a payment. Take the banker into your confidence early and he is more likely to become an ally than an adversary.
- **Behavior:** This is a business meeting. Treat it as you did your initial loan meeting. But this time, don't hesitate to respond somewhat aggressively to any bullying from the loan officer. You're still a supplicant, but you've got more leverage now that you owe the bank money.

# 19. Asking Institutional Lender to Recast Terms

**Icebreaker:** I'm finding it increasingly difficult to keep current in my loan because of a circumstance that has affected my stream of income. Shortly, I'll find it impossible. I think I have a solution, however. I came to you as soon as I knew.

**Reflexively negative:** *You're going to have to go elsewhere for help. You signed an agreement with us and you must fulfill your obligations.*

**Subtly aggressive:** I came here to try to avoid a default. That wouldn't be good for me and my credit, and you wouldn't want a defaulted loan on your books. I'd like to keep our relationship. The last thing I want to do is to have to plead my case to your boss. I think you and I can work this out together.

**Willing to listen:** *I'm not sure about that, but what did you have in mind?*

**Concerned:** *I'm sorry to hear that. What happened?*

**Offer explanation:** My income from my largest customer has been dramatically lowered and will remain so for the foreseeable future. They've had problems of their own and weren't able to help themselves. Accordingly, in order to pay this loan back I'll need to extend the term to six years rather than the three we had planned.

**Your fault?:** *That's all very well, but the bank is going to wonder why you couldn't have anticipated this happening and protected yourself.*

**Pitch:** We had cast this as a three-year loan, but with the externally created changes in my cash flow, I need to recast it as a six-year loan.

**Not my fault:** This is the first time they've disappointed me. There was no reason or circumstance where I could have guessed this would happen to them.

**Still hesitant:** *Look, it's not that simple. In effect you're asking for an entirely new loan. And your financial situation has obviously changed.*

**Will investigate:** *I don't know exactly what the bank's options are in this case. I'll have to see what I can do. I'll get back to you later in the week.*

**Ask for advice:** You're right. I guess what I'm really asking you for is advice. If you were me, how would you handle this?

**Ask for personal help:** I realize you can't do this on your own and you'll have to go to others. But I'd really appreciate it if you could be my advocate in this matter.

**Offers suggestion:** *What about if we keep it a three-year loan, but lower the payments to what they would be in a six-year loan and add a final balloon payment at the end? That would make the bank feel a lot more comfortable. You understand this isn't my decision. I'll have to talk to the lending committee.*

## ADAPTATIONS

This script can be modified to:

- Alter a pledge of time or effort to an institution
- Change the terms of an employment contract
- Revise the terms of an equipment or auto lease

## KEY POINTS

- Be businesslike, secure in your leverage, and confident in your business.
- If the banker shows concern, offer an explanation of your problem.
- If the banker is reflexively negative, feel free to show you know you've got some leverage.
- If the banker probes to see if you're at fault, demonstrate that the problem was unforeseeable and unavoidable.
- If the banker remains hesitant about your proposal, treat it as an offer to negotiate your proposal.
- Whether the banker offers an alternative plan or asks for time to prepare a response, ask him to serve as your advocate.

# Approaching a Family Lender

*20.*

## STRATEGY

If you're going to borrow money from friends or relatives for your business, it's best to make sure it's for the right reasons. That means money to expand, or buy new equipment. Funds borrowed from "friendly" lenders should be for things that add to the business, not as a way to get out of trouble. And loans shouldn't be for start-up money either—any such funds should be equity investments. The reasons for going to family and friends is that it may be less expensive than borrowing from an institutional source, the paperwork can be much less, and the terms can be much more flexible. For the friendly lender, such loans have benefits over other investments, including the possibility of tax advantages and equity options. It's best to approach someone who you know has liquid funds. Bring her, or her advisor, a proposal custom designed for her needs. Often, private individuals with the money to lend to a family member's business will have a financial advisor. Therefore, your goal in this dialogue might be to get her approval for you to speak with her advisor, and perhaps put in a good word for you.

## TACTICS

- **Attitude:** You're not looking for help, you're offering a proposal that's beneficial to both parties.
- **Preparation:** Be certain the individual has funds available. Have a potential deal in mind that has been customized for this individual's needs. If possible, have a third party, preferably another family member, serve as the source of the idea.
- **Timing:** Hold this meeting at a time convenient to the other party.
- **Behavior:** Break the ice with a telephone call first. Then meet the other party at her home to reinforce the personal ties you have. Be serious, but feel free to relate as you normally would. You aren't asking for help, you're proposing a mutually beneficial arrangement. However, dress as you would for a business meeting.

# 20. Approaching a Family Lender

**Icebreaker 1:** Hello, Aunt Sadie. This is Sheryl. I'm calling for a business reason today. I wanted to sit down with you and talk about a great opportunity I have. Uncle Henry suggested I speak with you. It would take too long to go over it on the telephone, so can I stop by to see you next Monday afternoon?

**Icebreaker 2:** Aunt Sadie, for years I've been trying to figure out ways for the business to grow bigger. You know we're paying for Junior's tuition at Yale and little Millie's piano lessons. What I've done is taken some steps to make the company bigger so we can make more money to pay for our growing needs. I was going to go to my bank to get a loan for this expansion program. But when I told Uncle Henry about what I was doing, he said it could be a wonderful financial opportunity for the family. I'd like to discuss that possibility with you.

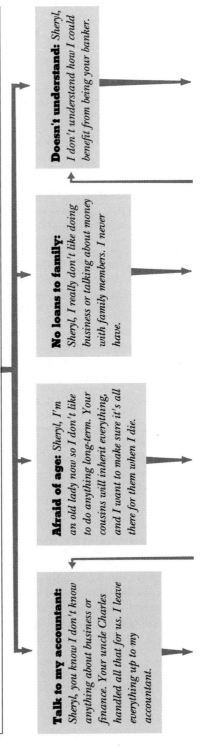

**Talk to my accountant:** *Sheryl, you know I don't know anything about business or finance. Your uncle Charles handled all that for us. I leave everything up to my accountant.*

**Afraid of age:** *Sheryl, I'm an old lady now so I don't like to do anything long-term. Your cousins will inherit everything, and I want to make sure it's all there for them when I die.*

**No loans to family:** *Sheryl, I really don't like doing business or talking about money with family members. I never have.*

**Doesn't understand:** *Sheryl, I don't understand how I could benefit from being your banker.*

**I'll do that:** I didn't expect you to make a financial or business analysis, Aunt Sadie. I'd be happy to speak with your accountant. I just wanted to speak with you first. Would you do me a favor and call them and let them know I'll be contacting them?

**Assuage fears:** That's something we can take care of, Aunt Sadie. We can make the loan payable on your death. Or if the kids like the terms and the way the company is doing they can extend the loan. We can leave it up to them.

**Are you sure?:** I hear what you're saying, Aunt Sadie. But why don't you look at it this way: Don't you think if we could both take advantage of a good deal we should do it, even though we're related?

**Explain concept:** We can structure a loan so it offers financial and tax advantages to both of us. . . . But I can talk to your accountant about the details.

**Still afraid:** *I don't know, Sheryl. I'm afraid. I just wouldn't feel comfortable doing something like this. I'm sorry.*

**I'll speak with accountant:** *Here's the telephone number of my accountant. I'll let him know you'll be calling.*

**Back off:** Don't be sorry, Aunt Sadie. I wouldn't want you to do anything that makes you uncomfortable. I love you. Why don't we have some tea?

**Thanks:** Thanks so much for listening to me, Aunt Sadie. I think this is something that could really help both of us. I'll give your accountant a call tomorrow morning.

## ADAPTATIONS

This script can be modified to:

- Borrow a substantial sum of money from a family member for a major personal investment, such as buying a home

## KEY POINTS

- Be sober, but personable.
- If she doesn't understand your idea, explain it simply.
- If she is fearful of age or estate factors, say that those can be accommodated.
- If she is leery of intrafamily business, say that it can be mutually beneficial.
- If she suggests you speak with an advisor, agree, but ask for an introduction.
- If she remains hesitant, back off and shift to an entirely personal visit.

# Asking a Family Lender to Recast Terms

*21.*

## STRATEGY

Sometimes there are unforeseen events that force entrepreneurs to alter their loan repayment schedules if they're to stay afloat. When the lender is a family member or friend, the request to recast terms is even more difficult than when the lender is an institution. That's because there's an added element of personal responsibility to the exchange that opens the borrower up to guilty feelings. The secret to this dialogue is realizing that your friendly creditors are, in this situation, no different than your institutional creditors. If you don't have the money to pay them back as planned they'll simply have to accept that and deal with it. Their only recourse is to sue you, and that will result in their not getting their full loan back, since it's likely to bankrupt the business. Still, you can't be so abrupt or direct with friends. Instead, let them vent, but keep discreetly steering them back to the fact that they have no option. Call every bluff, and deal directly with every threat. Eventually they'll have to back down. Of course, don't count on getting another loan from them in the future.

## TACTICS

- **Attitude:** Be compassionate and caring, but also realize you have all the leverage and there's really nothing they can rationally do other than accept the situation.
- **Preparation:** Have thorough documentation of the unforeseen and unavoidable occurrence, its impact on your finances, and your recast payback plan.
- **Timing:** Do this as soon as you know you'll have a problem meeting your payments, but not before you've had time to draft a new plan.
- **Behavior:** Even though you know you have all the leverage in this situation, don't be haughty. Address all their fears, anger, and worries to the extent possible. Offer to do all you can to help, but make it clear there's no way you can meet the previously agreed schedule and that you've exhausted all other options.

# 21. Asking a Family Lender to Recast Terms

**Icebreaker:** I have a serious problem I need to tell you about. I won't be able to pay the loan you made to me as quickly as I wanted to. My major customer has just gone bankrupt.

**Blames third party:** *Listen, I borrowed this money to lend it to you. It has to be paid back . . . as promised.*

**Show dismay:** If I had known you were borrowing the money I'd never have accepted it. I wouldn't have come to you unless I thought you had the money. I didn't know I was dealing with a third party.

**Don't get angry:** *Look, I just wanted to help you out. Don't get angry with me.*

**Needs money:** *What happened? I was counting on this money. Junior's tuition bills are coming up.*

**Didn't know:** I had no idea you were counting on this money for Junior's tuition. What do you want me to do? I simply don't have it.

**Seeks reassurance:** *You can't pay if you don't have it, but how do I know it won't happen again?*

**Issues threat:** *Hey, I want the money like you promised. If I don't get it I'll sue you for it.*

**Suing won't help:** I was hoping you wouldn't respond that way. If you sue and get a judgment it will just put me out of business because I don't have the money. It will help neither of us. Please reconsider.

**Blames spouse:** *My wife told me I shouldn't lend money to family (or) friends. She's never going to let me change the deal.*

**Reason with spouse:** If you explain to her that this has nothing to do with the health of the business or the quality of management, and that it's temporary, surely she'll understand.

**That won't help:** *No. That won't make any difference. She'll want the money back just as we'd agreed.*

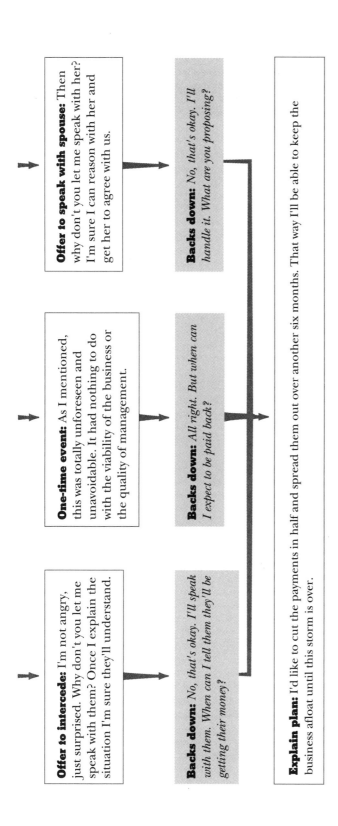

**Offer to intercede:** I'm not angry, just surprised. Why don't you let me speak with them? Once I explain the situation I'm sure they'll understand.

**Backs down:** *No, that's okay. I'll speak with them. When can I tell them they'll be getting their money?*

**One-time event:** As I mentioned, this was totally unforeseen and unavoidable. It had nothing to do with the viability of the business or the quality of management.

**Backs down:** *All right. But when can I expect to be paid back?*

**Offer to speak with spouse:** Then why don't you let me speak with her? I'm sure I can reason with her and get her to agree with us.

**Backs down:** *No, that's okay. I'll handle it. What are you proposing?*

**Explain plan:** I'd like to cut the payments in half and spread them out over another six months. That way I'll be able to keep the business afloat until this storm is over.

## ADAPTATIONS

This script can be modified to:

- Withdraw from a commitment to help a family member or friend

## KEY POINTS

- Be understanding, compassionate, and concerned on the exterior, but confident and secure on the interior.
- If he says there's a third party involved, show your dismay, and then offer to intercede.
- If he issues a threat, explain that such actions will help no one.
- If he stresses his need for the money, show understanding and concern, but reiterate that there's nothing you can do about the situation.
- If he blames his spouse, suggest reasoning with the spouse, and then offer to intercede.
- Launch into your plan only after the creditor has accepted that he has no choice but to accept a change in plans.

# Turning Down a Lender's Request for Equity in Your Company

22.

## STRATEGY

If you're doing poorly, the offer from a lender to take an equity position may be welcome. But if you're doing well, you're more likely to want to keep as much equity for yourself as you can. This creates a ticklish situation: you want to keep the lender on your side, but not give her what she wants. The best strategy is to make it clear that giving away equity would be a complicated process that might hinder your business's ability to thrive and keep paying her back.

## TACTICS

- **Attitude:** Take the request as a compliment. It reflects the lender's perception that you're doing well. But don't waver in your position that you "can't" (not "don't want to") give her equity.
- **Preparation:** Make a long list of all the other people who would be as deserving of equity as the lender. If you are following a formal business plan, have it with you.
- **Timing:** Respond to the request ASAP. This should not look like something you had to think about.
- **Behavior:** Hold this meeting in person to show that you have great respect for the lender and want to make sure she understands. Keep things friendly to stress that you're on the same team. Ask for agreement at every stage, and stop and thank the lender as soon as you have it.

# 22. Turning Down a Lender's Request for Equity in Your Company

**Icebreaker:** I'm flattered. Things are going well for all of us right now. But let's not tamper with something that's working.

**Not that simple:** It's not that simple. I'm following a formal business plan. It took me a long time to set my goals and determine my structure. I can't divert my attention and get into that process with lawyers and consultants again. I have to focus on my clients' business, not on reorganizing the company. Can't we just keep things the way they are?

**Not a big deal:** *This won't change anything. It's just that I can see you're doing well and I just want a piece of the action. It's not like I'll interfere.*

**Benefits others:** *Surely you're not going to turn down a cash infusion? I know your team would like to see bonuses.*

**Benefits you:** *C'mon. I've been watching you. You're going to burn yourself out. Take some money. Take a break. Live better. You've earned it!*

**Implicit contract:** *I've shared risks by lending you money as you were starting up. I want to share in the rewards, too.*

**Takes it personally:** *So, my money's not good enough for you now that you're doing fine?*

**Nothing personal:** This isn't personal. I'd give you an equity position as soon as I would any of the other special friends of the company who have asked—including my family, employees, lawyers, customers, suppliers, and a few others who have already asked me. But I have to tell you the same thing I told my parents. I'm focusing on the job of growing the business, and paying you, and to do that I need to keep things as they are. Okay?

**Your best interests:** You took the risk of lending me money because you saw that I had the entrepreneurial drive needed to make the business go and pay you back with interest. It's a great arrangement, and it's working. Diluting my stake might dilute my drive, which wouldn't be in your interests. Let's keep things on track, okay?

**Works best for me:** The current arrangement is best for me, thanks. I like working hard. I'm doing what I was meant to do. I don't want to take my eye off the ball and get involved in issues of distributing equity. I want to focus externally. I appreciate your concern, but let's keep the current arrangement, okay?

**Fairness:** What those others really want is equity in the company, just as you do. But, as I've told them, and my lawyer, my parents, and my biggest customer, the current arrangement is working—but it only works because I focus my energy and attention on customers, not on internal equity issues. You can imagine how unfair it would be to all of them, and how bad it would be for morale, if I gave you a piece of the pie and shut them out. You can appreciate that, can't you?

**Remains offended:** *I still don't think I'm asking for much, and I think you're shortchanging me.*

**Express thanks and close:** Your loans have been very important to us, and we appreciate that. But right now I'm doing what I said I couldn't do—spending a lot of business time on internal issues. I have to get back to work. Please excuse me. Thanks again for your offer.

**Agrees:** *I see your point—but I had to ask, and believe me, I'll ask again.*

**Express thanks:** Thank you for understanding how my business and I work.

## ADAPTATIONS

This script can be modified to:

- Turn down a customer's, supplier's, friend's, or relative's request for equity
- Turn down people who want you to enter into a joint venture with them
- Turn down people who want to take you public or franchise you

## KEY POINTS

- Stress that the current arrangement is working to everyone's benefit.
- If the lender implies that you owe her equity, cite all the other people who are equally deserving.
- After you answer each objection, ask for agreement.
- If she keeps pushing, end the conversation, in a friendly manner, by saying that you need to get back to work.

# Explaining Your Criminal Record to an Investor

23.

## STRATEGY

However a prospective investor finds out about your criminal record, from that point on there will be a suspicious air surrounding even the most civil of discussions. Suspicion could persist even after negotiations have been completed. Though it's unfair, you'll be held to the highest standards and subject to the lowest expectations. The goal of this lifescript is to show how your checkered past, far from a negative, is a positive: It's the most important life lesson you have experienced. Overcoming your failings has, in fact, made you a better person in general and a better businessperson in particular.

## TACTICS

- **Attitude:** Remain positive. This is just the kind of adversity that entrepreneurs must overcome if they're to succeed. Of course, having an attitude and action plan that exudes honesty and a forthright manner is absolutely critical.
- **Preparation:** Anticipation is essential in this lifescript. Of course you should have an impeccable business plan with a realistic and sweet projected return. But that's not enough in this situation. You'll also need a written factual account of the nature of your conviction. You need to set the stage so you can reframe or spin a different take on what a conviction typically implies.
- **Timing:** Have this discussion early in your relationship with an investor. It should be one presented as one of life's experiences that has brought you to this point, poised for incredible success. It's always better to bring it up yourself, but if you're ambushed, it's not a disaster.
- **Behavior:** Treat your criminal record as a fact of the past: history. It's not something to deny or feel embarrassed about, but it's also not something to be proud of or flippant about. Be pleasant but not boisterous, serious but not sullen, expressive but not emotional; keep hand motions small. In other words, be controlled and predictable.

# 23. Explaining Your Criminal Record to an Investor

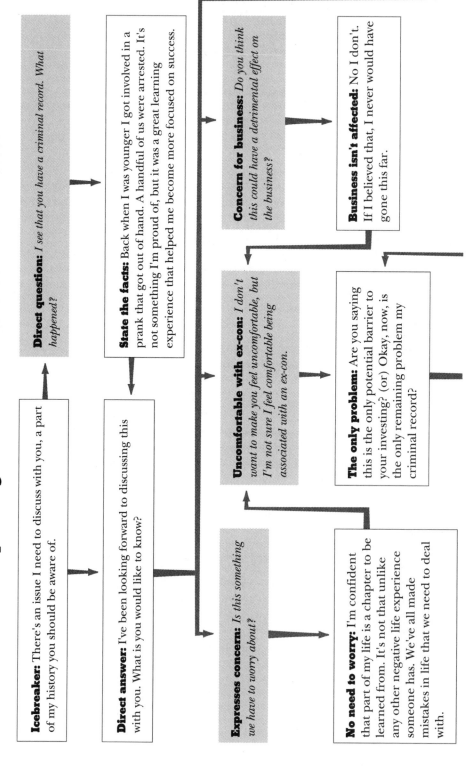

**Icebreaker:** There's an issue I need to discuss with you, a part of my history you should be aware of.

**Direct question:** *I see that you have a criminal record. What happened?*

**Direct answer:** I've been looking forward to discussing this with you. What is you would like to know?

**State the facts:** Back when I was younger I got involved in a prank that got out of hand. A handful of us were arrested. It's not something I'm proud of, but it was a great learning experience that helped me become more focused on success.

**Concern for business:** *Do you think this could have a detrimental effect on the business?*

**Business isn't affected:** No I don't. If I believed that, I never would have gone this far.

**Expresses concern:** *Is this something we have to worry about?*

**Uncomfortable with ex-con:** *I don't want to make you feel uncomfortable, but I'm not sure I feel comfortable being associated with an ex-con.*

**The only problem:** Are you saying this is the only potential barrier to your investing? (or) Okay, now, is the only remaining problem my criminal record?

**No need to worry:** I'm confident that part of my life is a chapter to be learned from. It's not that unlike any other negative life experience someone has. We've all made mistakes in life that we need to deal with.

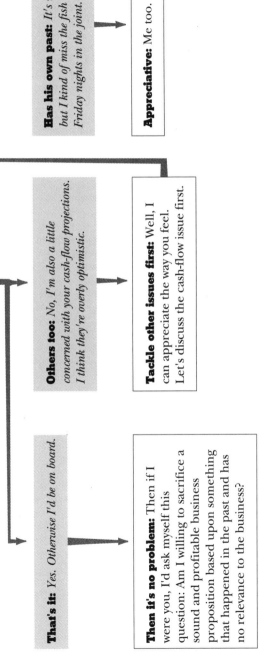

**Has his own past:** *It's nice to be out, but I kind of miss the fish dinners on Friday nights in the joint.*

**Appreciative:** Me too.

**Others too:** *No, I'm also a little concerned with your cash-flow projections. I think they're overly optimistic.*

**Tackle other issues first:** Well, I can appreciate the way you feel. Let's discuss the cash-flow issue first.

**That's it:** *Yes. Otherwise I'd be on board.*

**Then it's no problem:** Then if I were you, I'd ask myself this question: Am I willing to sacrifice a sound and profitable business proposition based upon something that happened in the past and has no relevance to the business?

## ADAPTATIONS

This script can be modified to:

- Turn just about any past indiscretion into a positive element

## KEY POINTS

- Treat this the same as all past indiscretions: a life lesson to be learned from and not repeated.
- Stress that surviving past challenges has made you stronger.
- Make sure that all else you do is beyond reproach—your internal standards should not even accept a white lie.
- Never assume what the potential investor's reaction will be.

# Inviting a Lender to Become Your Partner

## 24

## STRATEGY

People who have loaned you money are perfect prospects to ask for an equity investment. They already know who you are, already have a relationship with you, know your track record and, most importantly, *you* know *they* have the money. The best approach is to position your offer as an opportunity to take your relationship to a new level—one with a greater upside. You should not, however, rely too heavily on the relationship. Make sure you're offering them a genuine opportunity that they would want to pursue even if they had no experience with you, and present it with all the documentation you would normally use to support a proposal of this kind.

## TACTICS

- **Attitude:** You're happy to be able to present an opportunity that could be good for someone with whom you've had a positive business relationship.
- **Preparation:** Have a thoroughly documented, professionally prepared investment proposal that shows the projected return on the proposed investment. The proposal should show how an equity position is likely to be more rewarding than a loan.
- **Timing:** Approach your lender when you have all your documentation in order and—this is important—when your loan payments are up to date.
- **Behavior:** Hold the meeting in person, at the lender's place of business or home. Dress for a business meeting, even if the meeting is at a home.

# 24. Inviting a Lender to Become Your Partner

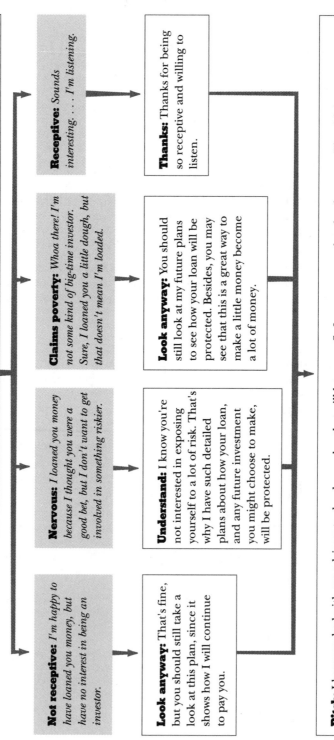

**Icebreaker:** I really appreciate the help you've given the company by lending us money. Now I'm ready to take the business to the next level. I want to share my new business plans with you, so you'll know how well your loans will be protected. At the same time, I want to offer you the opportunity to invest in our next stages of growth.

**Not receptive:** *I'm happy to have loaned you money, but have no interest in being an investor.*

**Nervous:** *I loaned you money because I thought you were a good bet, but I don't want to get involved in something riskier.*

**Claims poverty:** *Whoa there! I'm not some kind of big-time investor. Sure, I loaned you a little dough, but that doesn't mean I'm loaded.*

**Receptive:** *Sounds interesting . . . . I'm listening.*

**Look anyway:** That's fine, but you should still take a look at this plan, since it shows how I will continue to pay you.

**Understand:** I know you're not interested in exposing yourself to a lot of risk. That's why I have such detailed plans about how your loan, and any future investment you might choose to make, will be protected.

**Look anyway:** You should still look at my future plans to see how your loan will be protected. Besides, you may see that this is a great way to make a little money become a lot of money.

**Thanks:** Thanks for being so receptive and willing to listen.

**Pitch:** I have worked with my advisors to develop a plan that will let us profit from a new market development. The risk is minimal because it doesn't involve learning a new industry—just doing what we already do but on a larger scale. Working at this new level will be very rewarding for whoever provides me with the capital to get there. That's why I wanted to give you the first shot at this opportunity. Let me take you through the numbers. (Present the plan, stressing its conservative nature and a big, fast payoff.)

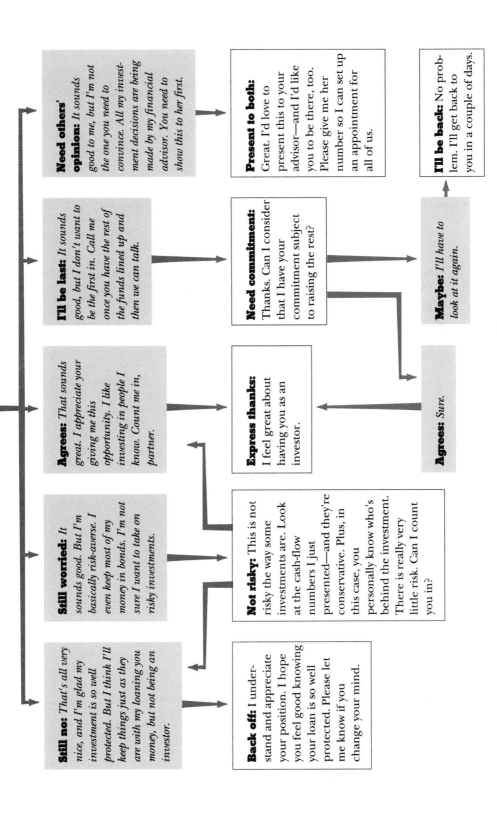

**Need others' opinion:** *It sounds good to me, but I'm not the one you need to convince. All my investment decisions are being made by my financial advisor. You need to show this to her first.*

**Present to both:** Great. I'd love to present this to your advisor—and I'd like you to be there, too. Please give me her number so I can set up an appointment for all of us.

**I'll be back:** No problem. I'll get back to you in a couple of days.

**I'll be last:** *It sounds good, but I don't want to be the first in. Call me once you have the rest of the funds lined up and then we can talk.*

**Need commitment:** Thanks. Can I consider that I have your commitment subject to raising the rest?

**Maybe:** *I'll have to look at it again.*

**Agrees:** *That sounds great. I appreciate your giving me this opportunity. I like investing in people I know. Count me in, partner.*

**Express thanks:** I feel great about having you as an investor.

**Agrees:** *Sure.*

**Still worried:** *It sounds good. But I'm basically risk-averse. I even keep most of my money in bonds. I'm not sure I want to take on risky investments.*

**Not risky:** This is not risky the way some investments are. Look at the cash-flow numbers I just presented—and they're conservative. Plus, in this case, you personally know who's behind the investment. There is really very little risk. Can I count you in?

**Still no:** *That's all very nice, and I'm glad my investment is so well protected. But I think I'll keep things just as they are with my loaning you money, but not being an investor.*

**Back off:** I understand and appreciate your position. I hope you feel good knowing your loan is so well protected. Please let me know if you change your mind.

## ADAPTATIONS

This script can be modified to:
- Ask a relative to invest
- Ask a supplier to invest
- Ask a customer to invest
- Ask a key employee to invest

## KEY POINTS

- Do not overstress your personal relationship. Make it clear that the proposal stands by itself.
- No matter what response you get to the icebreaker, steer the conversation to the pitch.
- If she is nervous about investing in general, separate this opportunity from other (riskier) investments.
- If she suggests you speak to a third party, treat it as an opportunity, ask that she be there, and schedule a meeting as soon as possible.
- If she continues to say no, don't push. Back off to preserve the relationship, and make it clear there are no hard feelings.

# Explaining a Prior Bankruptcy to a Prospective Investor

## 25.

### STRATEGY

Having filed for bankruptcy at some point in your past makes the tough situation of asking someone to invest even tougher. Your prior bankruptcy raises all kinds of questions about whether you're a good person to invest in. Nonetheless, there's no point in trying to hide the bankruptcy; that's likely to weaken your credibility even further. The best strategy is to disclose the bankruptcy up front and spin it as an experience you have learned from and are now prepared to prevent.

### TACTICS

- **Attitude:** Be frank and confident. Acknowledge that having been bankrupt is a liability, but be ready to counterbalance that liability with your more recent track record and your bright prospects.
- **Preparation:** Have all the documents relating to your bankruptcy, and a full set of documents attesting to your current fiscal fitness.
- **Timing:** Tell your prospective investors at the start of the process. It could be disastrous for them to find out about this from someone else.
- **Behavior:** Hold this meeting in person, at the lender's place of business or home. Dress for a business meeting, even if the meeting is at a home. Dress and act conservatively in order to reflect and project your stability.

# 25. Explaining a Prior Bankruptcy to a Prospective Investor

**Icebreaker and confession:** I'm really excited about having you as an investor, so I want to be sure that you, and all my other investors, have a full understanding of my plan and my qualifications. I have invested years in gaining the experience and knowledge needed to make this venture a success. It was a hard learning process, and at one point I even had to declare bankruptcy. But I learned from that experience and have compiled a flawless track record over the last ten years.

**Horrified automatic no:** *You declared bankruptcy once and you want me to invest in you? Not possible. I'm a very conservative investor and a blemish like that on your record automatically means I won't even look at you.*

**Cautious:** *Thank you for telling me. I hope you'll understand that it makes it very unlikely that I will invest.*

**Will bother others:** *I might be able to get past your bankruptcy, but I have very cautious partners. They won't be able to deal with it.*

**Understanding:** *I appreciate your honesty. I came close to bankruptcy once myself. I'll proceed carefully, as always, but I'm willing to hear your pitch, and it better be good.*

**An exception:** I respect your approach—caution is a good policy. But I think my particular case calls for an exception to that policy.

**Ask to meet with others:** I'd like to meet with your co-investors. I'm confident that when I explain all the circumstances, and show them all the evidence, they'll be more comfortable.

**Express thanks:** The presentation isn't just good, it's great, and the bankruptcy was an anomaly.

**Explanation:** My past bankruptcy was caused by a partner who cheated me (or whatever the explanation may be). I have all the court papers and accountants' reports here to show you. It was, of course, my fault for choosing a bad partner. But as you can see from my organizational chart, I have no partners in this venture except respectable investors like you. In light of that, are you ready to review the plan?

**Big no:** *Don't bother. I feel for you, getting taken and all that, but the bankruptcy is still a stumbling block for me.*

**Have to think about it:** *It sounds reasonable. But it's the kind of thing I have to sleep on. Let me get back to you about it.*

**Still need to check with others:** *That makes me feel better. But I still need to run it by my co-investors.*

**Green light:** *Okay. I believe in second chances—I'm on my third marriage. Let's see the plan.*

**Tactical temporary back-off:** I really want you as an investor. Could you please give some thought to what kind of documentation or assurances you would need to come on board, and I'll come by on Wednesday to discuss them with you?

**Offer documentation and reclaim initiative:** That's reasonable. Please take this presentation packet for your review. It's got all the documentation on my bankruptcy, testimonials to my recent performance and an executive summary of the projected returns my plan offers you. I'll come by on Wednesday to see if you have any questions.

**Press for meeting:** Great, but since this plan is my baby, I'd really like to present it to them in person. Can we arrange a meeting with all of us there? (At meeting, restart script from the top.)

**The plan:** Let's start with the projected returns. They are enormous, and you start receiving them very quickly. Now let's go on to. . . .

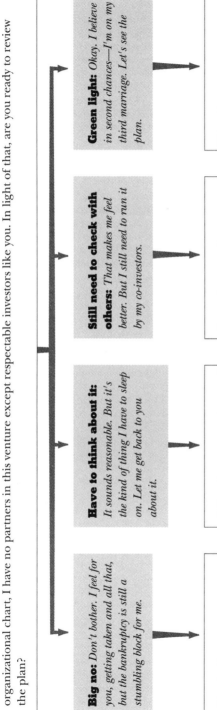

## ADAPTATIONS

This script can be modified to:
- Explain a prior bankruptcy to a prospective partner
- Explain a prior bankruptcy to a prospective supplier
- Explain a prior bankruptcy to a prospective customer
- Explain a prior bankruptcy to a prospective landlord

## KEY POINTS

- Have full documentation explaining the bankruptcy and why it won't happen again.
- No matter what response you get to the icebreaker and confession, steer the conversation to the explanation.
- Never make light of your bankruptcy, just explain why it will not reoccur.
- If the prospective investor suggests that coinvestors would be reluctant to invest, push for a meeting with them.
- If the investor remains reluctant, back off, but leave him with documentation, and tell him when you will schedule a follow-up meeting.

# III

# *Lifescripts*

## ...for Professionals, Suppliers, and Others

# Renegotiating Your Professional's Overcharge

*26.*

## STRATEGY

When you receive a surprisingly large bill from your professional, your first assumption should be that it's an error, either by the professional's staff or by her computerized billing system. Even if it's not a mistake, suggesting that one has happened gives your professional the chance to save face. Before you call, review all your records of what services you expected, and compare it to what the professional says she did. If more work was done than requested, it shouldn't be your responsibility. If the workload didn't increase, the professional made an error in her initial assessment and should have informed you of any changes while they were taking place. In either case, you shouldn't have to foot the bill. If the professional, either directly or indirectly, asks for more time, give it to her. She may need it to investigate and formulate her response.

## TACTICS

- **Attitude:** Be friendly and warm. Assume there's been a simple misunderstanding that can easily be resolved.
- **Preparation:** Review all your facts and records about the professional's services. Be clear about what you were prepared, or told to expect, to pay. Check whether there were any "emergencies." Expect the professional to become defensive.
- **Timing:** Respond as soon as you receive the bill. Prompt attention will show the professional that you review bills closely and aren't afraid of asking questions.
- **Behavior:** Feel free to have this conversation over the telephone. Treat the professional as your equal, not your superior or your supplicant. Stress the implied understanding you had about what the bill would be.

# 26. Renegotiating Your Professional's Overcharge

**Icebreaker:** Hi, Jane. I just received your bill for $2,000 and I wanted to call right away. I'm sure there must be some clerical error or misunderstanding. The invoice was way out of line with the amount you had told me to expect.

**Wants time 1:** *Look, Diane, I can't deal with this right now. I'll have someone get back to you later today.*

**Wants time 2:** *Look, Diane, I'm tied up right now. I'll look into it myself and get back to you later today.*

**Conciliatory:** *What exactly is the problem with the bill?*

**Defensive:** *I don't think there's an error. I dictate and personally review all the bills before they go out.*

**Deal with you:** I appreciate your looking into this, Jane. Of course, because my dealings were with you personally, I'd appreciate discussing this will you rather than someone on your staff.

**Misunderstanding:** I'm sure it has just been some kind of misunderstanding that we'll be able to clear up.

**Question amount of work:** I've gone over the nature of the work and I don't see how it could have taken more than ten hours of your time. I know you bill at a rate of $100 an hour but that leads to a total of $1,000, well under the $2,000 you billed.

**Question estimate:** I need you to review your records. Based on our initial conversations I assumed the bill would be between $1,000 and $1,500. You never told me that things had changed.

**I'll be back:** If I don't hear from you by (three days later), I'll give you another call.

**Please clarify:** Help me understand what happened. The work I asked for couldn't possibly take more than ten hours. Did you provide more services than I asked for? (or) The final estimate I got from you was for $1,000. Did something happen to change that, and if so, why didn't you tell me about it?

**Stands ground:** *Regardless of your estimates or recollections, the bill is accurate. I spent fifteen hours on the project. I bill at $100 an hour. And I incurred $500 in expenses.*

**Backs off:** *You're right. There must have been a mistake somewhere in the process. The bill should be adjusted to $1,250. Are you comfortable with that number?*

## ADAPTATIONS

This script can be modified to:
- Question a friend who has spent more than was agreed on a joint gift
- Question anyone who goes beyond the parameters you've outlined

## KEY POINTS

- Some type of mistake was made, otherwise you wouldn't have been surprised by the bill.
- Give the professional time to formulate a response or to investigate.
- Insist on dealing personally with the professional.
- Be open to offers at compromise.
- If pushed, make it clear the professional has made a mistake of omission or commission.

# Asking your Professional to Reduce His or Her Fee

27.

## STRATEGY

It's easy to ask a professional who's making mistakes or giving you bad service to reduce his fee—you have little to lose if he quits. But it's much harder to ask a professional whom you respect and whose work you value to reduce his fee. You have to manage the conversation so your request does not cause him to quit or serve you less well. The best approach is to blame external factors for the need to ask for a reduced fee and, at the same time, stress the long-term benefits of a continued working relationship with you.

## TACTICS

- **Attitude:** Be prepared for the possibility of (justifiable) anger. Make it clear you regret having to make this request.
- **Preparation:** Make absolutely sure you must make this request; it's not one to make lightly. Have the facts about your financial situation at your fingertips. Know which outside force you're going to blame for the situation: creditors, accountant, investors, consultants, ex-spouse, and so on.
- **Timing:** Have this conversation as soon as it's clear this is absolutely necessary. The sooner you have it, the sooner your fees will go down.
- **Behavior:** Go to the professional's office. You're asking a big favor; don't make him travel, too. As always, stop and thank the professional the minute he has agreed.

# 27. Asking your Professional to Reduce His or Her Fee

**Icebreaker:** I'm at a crucial make-or-break time in my business. I've just met with my accountant, and he has dictated an emergency survival plan for me.

**Pitch:** He has told me that I have to ask all the professionals who serve me to take a 20 percent cut in their fees. He personally volunteered to take a 30 percent cut, and I have cut my draw by 40 percent and am living on an austerity budget. I'll return your fees to today's level as soon as I can, but for now I have to ask you to charge less.

**Suggests alternatives:** *That's ridiculous. Don't cut him back 30 percent—fire him altogether. You don't cut back on your professionals just because you hit a tough spot. That's when you need us most. Borrow some money, or pay your suppliers more slowly.*

**Takes it personally:** *What have I done wrong? I thought you liked me. I thought we had chemistry. You keep complimenting my work. What happened? Have you met another designer?*

**Gets angry:** *That's an insult. That's less than my son makes washing cars. There's lots of business out there for an experienced professional like me. What happened to all that respect you used to talk about?*

**Accepts:** *Okay. It's a good thing I like you. But you're going to owe me one, big time.*

**Reject alternatives:** I wish it were that simple. But I've already stretched my suppliers as far as I can, and I need to reflect lower professional fees in order to have a business plan I can take to the bank to get some interim funds. I wouldn't make this request if there was any way I could avoid it.

**Not personal:** Please—I think you're wonderful. I'm still your biggest fan, and the best person you could send prospects to for recommendations. I want to work with you forever. This has nothing to do with you. It's all about the financial mess I'm in.

**Absorb anger and plead relationship:** You have every right to react that way. It is a rotten thing that I have to ask you to do. As you can imagine, I feel horrible having to ask this. I know you're worth your fee, and I've turned down lots of offers from people who would charge less. But right now I have no choice but to ask you to reduce your fee.

**Express thanks:** Thank you. This means a lot to me.

**Restate with added concern and commitment:** I am at a critical point. I hate having to ask this. I know it's unfair to you but I have no choice. All I can do is promise to bring you back up to an appropriate level as soon as I can, and promise to give you the same glowing recommendations that have helped you grow your business. Can you please reduce the fee you charge me by 20 percent?

**Reject deal, offer commitment:** I can't agree to that, and I value you too much to make false promises. I have been put on a strict no-nonsense plan and I don't have that leeway. All I can do is promise to put your fees back up as soon as they let me and continue to give you the world's greatest recommendations in the meantime. Can you meet me there? I can't help thinking that you might do just as well sticking with me at a lower fee as you will spending a lot of money and energy pitching a new account.

**Negotiates:** *I'll go along with this nonsense as long as you promise it's only for three months and you agree to pay me back the difference between what I would have made and what I will make at the lower rate in the first quarter that you are profitable.*

**Resigns your account:** *I can't work for 20 percent less. I'll have to move on at the end of the month.*

**Show regret and leave the door open:** I am, of course, disappointed, but I understand. But it's your decision. Please don't lose touch. I expect to be back in the black soon and would love to resume our business relationship then.

**Accepts commitment:** *I'm not crazy about it, but I'll stick with you.*

## ADAPTATIONS

This script can be modified to:
- Temporarily reduce an employee's salary or wage
- Temporarily reduce a child's allowance
- Temporarily reduce the amount of work given to a vendor

## KEY POINTS

- Focus the discussion on the inevitability of the situation.
- If he suggests compromise, say it's impossible.
- If he gets angry, absorb the anger.
- If he takes it personally, stress it is about you, not him.
- After you answer each objection, ask for agreement.
- If you are unable to get agreement, leave the door open.

# Explaining an Understatement of Income to the IRS

*28.*

## STRATEGY

If an IRS auditor discovers that you've underreported your income, you must respond quickly and establish that the understatement was an oversight on your part, not a deliberate act of fraud. Your goal is to admit the error immediately and dutifully pay the appropriate tax and penalty without giving the IRS reason to tie you up in an audit covering other areas or other years.

## TACTICS

- **Attitude:** Treat this as a serious matter, regardless how small the amount involved. You need to demonstrate clearly your desire and intention to pay your taxes properly. Remember the examiner is just doing her job. She has no reason to persecute you unless you give her one.
- **Preparation:** Prepare to address fully the issue the IRS specifies in its written notice to you. Be ready to write a check and settle the matter on the spot. Have baby or pet pictures in your wallet if that will help explain how you missed that piece of income when you were doing your taxes.
- **Timing:** Since you're not going to dispute the issue, let the IRS examiner determine the timing.
- **Behavior:** Go to the IRS office in order to keep the attention focused on the one issue in question. Treat your IRS examiner as a teacher or coach. Let her lead the conversation—as long as she sticks to the specific area of inquiry. Do not volunteer any information that isn't specifically requested.

# 28. Explaining an Understatement of Income to the IRS

**Icebreaker:** I checked on the income you mentioned in your notice and you're absolutely right, I totally forgot about it. I feel terribly embarrassed. What's the best way for me to correct this oversight?

**Verifies:** *So you agree you received this income yet did not report it?*

**Contrite confession:** Oh no. You're absolutely right about this. I was so scatterbrained after Junior was born that I completely missed this income. What should I do?

**Probes:** *Do you have any other unreported income? Is there anything else we should know?*

**Concerned denial:** I certainly don't think so. After I got your notice I went over every scrap of paper the puppy hadn't chewed. As far as I can tell, this is the only thing that fell through the cracks. What should I do?

**Instructs:** *You need to file a revised return. (or) You can sign this statement and pay right now.*

**Eager agreement:** Fine. I'll do whatever it takes to correct this. I'd like to set things straight as soon as possible.

## ADAPTATIONS

This script can be modified to:
- Deal with municipal inspectors who have discovered a code violation
- Deal with a condo or co-op board that has discovered you're in violation of their rules
- Deal with an animal control officer who discovers your dog is unlicensed

## KEY POINTS

- Admit your oversight and ask the examiner how you can resolve the matter.
- Call it an "oversight."
- If she tries to broaden the discussion, steer it back to the situation specified in the notice and ask for a solution.
- If she keeps trying to broaden the discussion, stand up, ask for an adjournment, and return only with your tax advisor or attorney.

# Explaining an Overstatement of Expenses to the IRS

## 29

## STRATEGY

Even though there's great latitude in the interpretation of what is deductible, your first objective will be to settle the matter as quickly as possible. An ongoing dialogue with the IRS will eat up not only a lot of your valuable time, but your stomach lining as well. Go over the expenses the IRS brings up. Stand by them only if you are certain each is legitimate and you have adequate documentation. In all other cases, accept their interpretations and/or provide new, fully documented numbers. Make it clear that you had thought the deductions were legitimate, or that you thought you had documentation for them. Now that you understand, the mistake will not be repeated.

## TACTICS

- **Attitude:** Treat this as a serious matter, no matter how small the amount involved. Convey your earnest desire to set things straight. Treat the IRS examiner with respect. Show that you understand he has power and he won't feel the need to demonstrate it.
- **Preparation:** Decide whether your claimed deductions are both legitimate and fully documented. If not, prepare new, completely defensible numbers. If they are, prepare a package outlining your defense.
- **Timing:** As long as you have adequate time to prepare you can let the IRS examiner set the time for the meeting.
- **Behavior:** Remain sincere, professional, and nonconfrontational. Let the IRS examiner do most of the talking. Do not volunteer any information that isn't specifically requested.

# 29. Explaining an Overstatement of Expenses to the IRS

**Icebreaker:** I see from your notice that you're questioning my deductions for last year. Could you please tell me which deductions you're questioning so we can discuss them?

**Full review:** *All of them. Your return is outside of our guidelines and was red flagged. I'm going to need to see backup for all your deductions. Let's start with your cellular telephone and monthly cell phone service.*

**Specific problem:** *I'm interested in your cellular telephone bills. You've deducted the entire cost rather than a percentage.*

**Agree:** Okay, let me show you the receipts (you have no choice but to agree).

**Polite disagreement:** Your questioning my cell phone bills surprises me. I specifically checked with my accountant and he said that since I only use the cell phone to talk to my clients that it would be valid. I'm sure you'll allow the deduction when you've had a chance to look at these records.

**Bureaucratic strong arm:** *We'll disallow it for the moment.*

**Surprised agreement:** Really? I'm sorry. I thought we had separated out the handful of personal calls. Well, you're the expert on the tax code, so I'll go along with what you say.

**Offers compromise:** *As long as you agree to my other points I can let that deduction stand.*

**Presents bill:** *In total you owe an additional $11,235, plus $2,879 in interest and penalties.*

**Reluctant agreement:** Gee, that seems like a lot, but I really have to get back to work. Every minute I sit here with you I risk losing customers. Is there some way I can pay over time without incurring more interest and penalties?

**Protest:** While I agree with much of what you've said, I can't agree with your disallowing my cell phone deduction. I need it for my business and only use it for business calls. I'd like to settle this today. Can we discuss this issue with your supervisor?

## ADAPTATIONS

This script can be modified to:

- Explain bills questioned by clients
- Explain a schedule of needs submitted to a bankruptcy or divorce court

## KEY POINTS

- Discuss only the deductions he questions.
- Agree, don't admit.
- Go along where you feel you can.
- Ask about a payment schedule.
- When you must disagree, do so politely.
- Stress your desire to settle the issue and ask for an immediate chance to appeal.

# Explaining Your Lack of Good Credit to a Supplier

30.

## STRATEGY

Always remember: A supplier's livelihood is due in large part to granting credit to customers. Somewhere there's a vendor willing to sell product to even the most credit-beleaguered business. Your goal is to convince this supplier she will miss the opportunity to establish loyalty with your soon-to-be successful business. You do this by explaining that your creditworthiness should be based not only on history, but on present and future business viability as well. Rationalize why your credit history is the way it is, and explain what has occurred, or will occur, to ensure she will not end up with the short stick. You want this vendor to feel she's an important part of your business, and that you're on the verge of the profitability and stability that will lead to increased sales of her product. Suggest that by denying you credit the supplier may lose you as a customer forever, and by the same token if she chooses to grant you credit she has assured herself of a loyal customer.

If your efforts fail, that need not be the end. Offer to pay higher interest with shorter terms for a specific period of time—six months at most—at which point the agreement reverts back to normal terms and the difference in interest rates is rebated as a credit toward future purchases. Offer to pay cash on delivery—again for a specific amount of time. Be creative. Finally, leave the door open for future consideration. If you reapply every six months, just the fact that you're still in business and are reminding the supplier by your persistence may be enough to get you the credit you want.

## TACTICS

- **Attitude:** Convey enthusiasm and confidence, tempered with modesty. Don't be desperate, apologetic, or arrogant. The belief that your business will be successful and that the supplier will be able to reap the rewards of that success are the key elements for a convincing presentation.
- **Preparation:** Be prepared to show what has happened and what will happen to make your business successful. Have real documented evidence in the form of a business plan and specific business or industry information that may have been responsible for injuring your credit. Also include any proof of future revenue such as purchase orders, accounts receivable and method of collection, investor dollars that may be on their way, and any other cash-generating elements. If you can't gather such information perhaps you should be looking at the viability of your business.

123

# 30. Explaining Your Lack of Good Credit to a Supplier

**Icebreaker:** We've been refining our business plan. In reviewing the elements needed for success, we've noticed our lack of good credit may be a challenge to what we're capable of accomplishing. I'm sharing this information with you, and with our other sources, because I'd appreciate input on credit matters. That would position all of us to benefit from the company's new profitable direction.

**Ambushed:** *In reviewing your account (or) application, we've found your credit is not good. It's cause for us to have concern.*

**Take charge:** I'm glad you've brought this up because we're in the process of revising our business plan based on the future potential and new opportunities we are seeing in the market. In reviewing our information, credit has been part of our discussions. We don't want this to affect our relationship with a quality vendor that has (or could have) an impact on the profitability potential of this company.

**Unimpressed:** *That's great. I'm glad you're looking at your business and trying to improve it, but we're unable to carry you. We just can't afford to put ourselves in that position.*

**Empathetic, not defensive:** I understand. We have a few of those types of customers ourselves. But we found that by looking at each instance individually we reclaimed some incredibly strong clients who, because of unique circumstances, didn't conform to the ideal profile on paper. I'd like to share our revised business plan with you. Also, we'd be willing to consider paying a higher interest rate.

**Not willing to reconsider:** *Look, I can appreciate what you're saying but we can't be the ones to take a chance on your poor credit.*

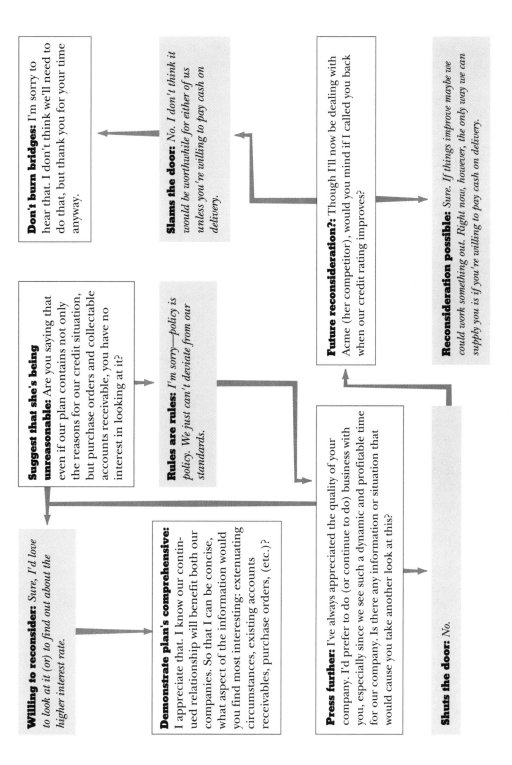

**Don't burn bridges:** I'm sorry to hear that. I don't think we'll need to do that, but thank you for your time anyway.

**Slams the door:** *No. I don't think it would be worthwhile for either of us unless you're willing to pay cash on delivery.*

**Future reconsideration?:** Though I'll now be dealing with Acme (her competitor), would you mind if I called you back when our credit rating improves?

**Reconsideration possible:** *Sure. If things improve maybe we could work something out. Right now, however, the only way we can supply you is if you're willing to pay cash on delivery.*

**Suggest that she's being unreasonable:** Are you saying that even if our plan contains not only the reasons for our credit situation, but purchase orders and collectable accounts receivable, you have no interest in looking at it?

**Rules are rules:** *I'm sorry—policy is policy. We just can't deviate from our standards.*

**Willing to reconsider:** *Sure, I'd love to look at it (or) to find out about the higher interest rate.*

**Demonstrate plan's comprehensive:** I appreciate that. I know our continued relationship will benefit both our companies. So that I can be concise, what aspect of the information would you find most interesting: extenuating circumstances, existing accounts receivable, purchase orders, (etc.)?

**Press further:** I've always appreciated the quality of your company. I'd prefer to do (or continue to do) business with you, especially since we see such a dynamic and profitable time for our company. Is there any information or situation that would cause you to take another look at this?

**Shuts the door:** *No.*

- **Timing:** If you wait until you're desperate, you'll be at a distinct disadvantage. Try to anticipate the suppliers you will need to approach, such as those you'll need to grow your business, and competitors of existing vendors to protect yourself from price gouging when you're down. Approach vendors early and most will recognize the good business sense you are exhibiting, helping diminish concerns about your business acumen.
- **Behavior:** Make it clear your poor credit is part of the past—it's history, not an indication of future business success. Be enthusiastic and confident—act as though the difficult past has honed your skills and your resolve. Don't be overconfident, however. Business failures are often created by the overconfidence and unwillingness of an entrepreneur to listen to the advice of other people. The price of credit in this instance may very well be to listen to the accumulated knowledge of an experienced supplier. Give it a try—you may learn something.

## ADAPTATIONS

This script can be modified to:
- Close the deal with a reluctant investor
- Borrow money, again, from a reluctant friend or family member

## KEY POINTS

- Remain calm, professional, enthusiastic, and positive about your business's future success.
- Do not be defensive, apologetic, or arrogant.
- Remember: A supplier's livelihood depends on granting credit.
- There's always another source.
- Poor credit in the past is not an absolute prediction of the future, nor an indication of a poor business or poor business acumen.
- Make developing a relationship with the supplier your goal.
- Make your supplier feel a part of the success of your business.
- Anticipate problems by having tough conversations and negotiations before it becomes critical.
- Present the reality that your business is poised for profitability and growth.
- Don't burn bridges. Things change.

# Asking a Supplier for a Consignment Deal

*31.*

## STRATEGY

Your strategy in asking for a consignment deal is dictated by the supplier. If the supplier is a large organization, you don't have much leverage. Of course, it does want to sell its products, so there's some room to negotiate. Explain that your business can't afford to pay for products on a normal payment schedule. Once you begin selling the supplier's products, and are generating enough money, you can pay for monthly orders on time. Initially, however, you need a consignment deal. A good salesperson will understand the importance of beginning a relationship with a new distributor and might agree to work on consignment. The salesperson may also want to compromise, suggesting a percentage agreement, whereby you'll receive a discount based on timely payments. The specifics of each offer will be different, so be prepared to haggle in order to reach a mutually beneficial agreement.

If the supplier is a small company, you have much more leverage. The supplier is under pressure to sell products and will be ready to compromise if it means getting items into your store. Explain that you like the products, but are unsure of demand and of whether your customers will pay the suggested price. Consignment allows you to ascertain market value and customer demand for the products. The supplier will want you to stock the items, so you should be reluctant to compromise. In either scenario, feel out the supplier and see how much latitude he will offer you.

## TACTICS

- **Attitude:** Be professional and swift. If facing a large supplier, establish a friendly tone and be open to compromises. Be firm with a small supplier, since he needs you a lot more than you need him. It's a consignment deal or nothing.
- **Timing:** You most likely will not dictate the timing, but be accommodating to the other party. If he calls to make an appointment, try to fit his schedule. It will ease the tension surrounding negotiations.
- **Preparation:** Research each supplier and know what companies will come to your store selling products. If you can learn about each company in advance, you'll be more prepared when it comes time to negotiate.

# 31. Asking a Supplier for a Consignment Deal

**Icebreaker:** I'm impressed with the quality of your inventory and would like to stock your products, but I have some reservations. I'd like to work on consignment.

**Pitch a large supplier:** I don't have enough cash for a purchase. If I could work on a consignment deal, then I'd be able to sell your products and you'll make money as soon as I do.

**Pitch a small supplier:** I'm not sure my customers will pay your prices or demand your product. It's too much of a risk for me to invest in your inventory. I'll stock your products, but we need to have a consignment deal.

**Large company compromise:** *Well, my company doesn't allow consignment deals. However, I would like to work out something. What if I give you forty-five days to pay back the outstanding debt?*

**Large company no:** *I'm sorry, my company doesn't allow me to work on consignment. I'll leave my card and when your financial situation improves we can talk about a purchase.*

**Small company no:** *Being a small company, we really count on sales to make money. I'd really prefer to have a normal purchase agreement. Perhaps you could make a small order? The risk for you would be minimal and it would prove the marketability of my products.*

**Small company agreement:** *Okay, consignment sounds reasonable. I understand your position and appreciate your stocking my products. If all goes well, maybe we can arrange for a normal payment plan in the future.*

**Haggle:** I understand your position and appreciate your offer, but I need a consignment deal. It simply comes down to dollars and cents. If you work with me now and the product performs well, I may be able to place future orders on a normal payment schedule.

**Negotiate:** I understand your company's policy, but I think there's an opportunity here for both of us to profit. How about consignment for the first order only? If all goes well, I'll agree to future orders with a normal payment schedule.

**No deals:** I'm hesitant to pay for products without any prior knowledge of their performance. I hope we'll be able to work out a consignment deal, because otherwise I don't think I can stock your products.

**No promises:** I'm glad we'll be stocking your products, but I can't make any promises about future orders. Let's just take this one month at a time.

**Let's make a deal:** *All right, I'm willing to make a deal. I'll work on consignment, if you agree to place an order next month and pay on a normal schedule. If you agree to my terms, I'll agree to yours.*

**No haggle:** *My company just won't let me deviate from the rules. I can offer you a forty-five-day window of payment. I'm not permitted to offer anything further.*

**Agree:** That sounds reasonable. Next month, I'll pay for the order within the normal time frame. I'm glad we could work this out.

**Take a month:** I'm sorry to hear that. Maybe you could come back next month when circumstances may be different. It's just a bad time now, but I'd like to work together in the future.

- **Behavior:** When facing a large supplier, assure the salesperson that you're seeking a long-term relationship, but need to start with a consignment deal. When facing a smaller supplier, be indifferent. Explain that you'll only stock his products with a consignment deal. Depending on the product sales performance you may adjust later, but make no promises.

## ADAPTATIONS

This script can be modified to:
- Ask for a loan with an open-ended due date for payment
- Ask for an investment with no guarantee of payment

## KEY POINTS

- Know the size of your supplier and negotiate accordingly.
- With a larger supplier, press for a consignment deal, but be ready to compromise.
- With a smaller supplier, it's a consignment deal or nothing. Don't make any promises regarding future purchases.
- If you can't reach an agreement, suggest another meeting in a month or two. Keep the lines of communication open.

# Asking a Supplier for a Special Credit Accommodation

*32.*

## STRATEGY

When negotiating for a credit accommodation, you need to stand your ground. A salesperson is often under pressure to meet quotas and eager to establish future relationships with distributors. Explain that you like the products, but need a credit incentive to make the purchase affordable. Most suppliers offer a standard 2 percent discount for payment received in thirty days. Asking for more time forfeits your right to a small discount, but your goal is to extend your credit time limit. Try suggesting sixty days as a deadline for payment. You're asking for something a little out of the ordinary, so you might have to settle for a forty-five-day credit. If the salesperson protests, tell her sixty days provides you with time to sell the product and earn money from the sales to pay the bill. If the salesperson is unmoved by your reasoning, and you really want to stock the product, you can offer to make a deal: If you're granted a sixty-day credit, then on the next order you'll agree to the standard thirty-day payment plan. This assures the salesperson of making two sales and you receive the credit accommodation for the first month. Another compromise is suggesting a forty-five-day credit. It might not be exactly what you want, but it should seal the deal. Try to force the salesperson to make the first move and negotiate credit terms from that point.

## TACTICS

- **Attitude:** Don't show too much emotion. You don't want the salesperson to know what you're thinking. Tell her you need the credit accommodation—that's the bottom line.
- **Timing:** Try to meet at a mutually conducive time for both of you. If possible, accommodate the salesperson's suggested time for discussing a sale.
- **Preparation:** Research the supplier as much as possible. Ask other distributors about past experiences with negotiations. Find out everything you can about the company's sales policies prior to speaking with the salesperson. Be sure you're speaking to someone empowered to make a deal.
- **Behavior:** Keep the meeting friendly and cordial. You're trying to establish a working relationship, not annoy a prospective supplier. No matter how it turns out, keep the tone positive.

# 32. Asking a Supplier for a Special Credit Accommodation

**Icebreaker:** I'm interested in stocking your products, but we need to speak about a credit accommodation. I know the standard procedure is payment in thirty days, but I need a little more time. If you could extend my credit to sixty days, I think we have a deal.

**Make a deal:** *I'll tell you what. I'll extend you a credit to sixty days, but you need to agree to the standard payment plan on future orders. The only way I can get you a special credit is if you meet me halfway.*

**Feeling you out:** *I'm not sure I can do that. Exactly what kind of purchase order are we talking about? If you tell me what you have in mind, maybe we can make a deal.*

**No:** *My company doesn't allow extended credit. I can offer the thirty-day credit, but I can't extend to sixty. I'm sorry, that's our policy.*

**Feel her out:** I'm not sure I can promise additional orders just yet. I want to see how your product sells with my customers. If everything works out, then I'll want to place additional orders. For starters, however, I'd like one order with a sixty-day credit accommodation.

**Don't show your hand:** Well, initially, I'd like to place an order and monitor the performance of your product for sixty days. If I have two months to test the market, I can make a decision on future purchases. However, I need the sixty-day credit to make the initial purchase.

**Stand your ground:** That's too bad. I'd really like to stock your products, but I need a sixty-day credit until the product starts selling. Are you sure there's no way for you to make a deal? I'm certain your company will be pleased to acquire a long-term customer.

**Stonewall:** *I'm sorry, I just can't extend your credit. Thirty days is the best I can do. If you can't live with that, I don't think I can sell you any products. Sorry.*

**See you next month:** I'm sorry to hear that. I just can't handle anything right now except on a sixty-day credit. I hope you understand. Maybe we can do business in the future. Thanks again.

**Eager to deal:** *All right, you got me. I'll agree to one order with a sixty-day credit. Provided our products sell well, and I know they will, I hope we can do business in the future. I'll call you periodically to see how sales are going.*

**Compromise:** All right, how about a forty-five-day credit? It might be tight, but I think I'll be able to pay the bill in six weeks. Meet me halfway at forty-five days and we have a deal.

**Deal:** *All right, that sounds fair. I'll start the paperwork on your order right away. I look forward to working with you.*

## ADAPTATIONS

This script can be modified to:

- Negotiate a leasing agreement with a salesperson
- Strike a payment deal with a credit card company

## KEY POINTS

- Try to force the salesperson to make the first move.
- Don't agree to any counterdemands too quickly. The salesperson may agree to your conditions without haggling or compromising.
- Hint that you'll be interested in future purchases if you get the sixty-day credit.
- If you really like the products and want to stock them, agree to a compromise.
- If you can't reach a deal, keep the lines of communication open. Suggest meeting in a month or two to discuss the matter again.

# Turning Down Employee Requests for Equity in the Firm

**33.**

## STRATEGY

Every few weeks another article appears about how many young employees have become multimillionaires through their equity stake in Microsoft, and employees at companies of all sizes start angling for equity. Even if your company is still in debt and all they'd be getting is a share of a negative number, they're still being prompted to ask for a stake. It's relatively easy to turn down one of many employees, or a marginal performer. The challenge is how to say no to a key employee in a small company. The best strategy is to stress that your turning down his request for equity reflects the difficulty of rearranging the ownership of the company. Tell him you value him and he figures prominently in your future plans. You may also want to promise that no broad redistribution of equity will happen without taking care of the handful of key employees who stick with you.

## TACTICS

- **Attitude:** Be very concerned and responsive. The quality of your response may have a big impact on whether your key employee starts looking for opportunities at other companies or thinking about becoming a competitor.
- **Preparation:** While it would be great to have done extensive homework before having this conversation, it's more important to respond quickly. Give some quick thought to just how valuable the employee is to you. If the employee is essential, you may want to make a commitment about his being included in future equity distributions.
- **Timing:** Respond to the request quickly. The urgency with which you respond will emphasize how much you value the employee. It's best to settle the matter quickly and get the employee focused on his job (not his career) again.
- **Behavior:** Hold the meeting at a time and a place that show it's important to you, perhaps at an upscale restaurant or on a golf course, if that's your style.

# 33. Turning Down an Employee's Requests for Equity in Your Company

**Icebreaker and denial:** Your request for equity made it clear we need to have a talk. It's a perfectly appropriate request, but we just can't do it right now. It would take too much time and too much in the way of legal fees. But I need you to know I value your contributions to the company and will take care of you as soon as I can.

**Repeats request:** *Give me a break. It can't be that complicated, and you're talking to the lawyers day and night already. You can do it.*

**Complicated:** Actually, it is that complicated. Not just the new papers and filings, but all the people who would have to be stoked. The lawyers you mentioned have also hit me up for equity, not to mention various customers, suppliers, lenders, accountants, consultants, relatives, and lawyers for my ex-wife. I can't open that can of worms now. I need to keep both of us focused on building the business so there can be a really big payday for both of us down the road.

**Need motivation:** *Since when have we shied away from complications? I'm killing myself for you. I'm working eighty-hour weeks. I can't psyche myself up for it unless there's a bigger prize than a salary in the picture.*

**Need a path:** *So it's awkward. So is explaining my hours to my kids. I'm building all sorts of value for you. I'm at a stage in my life where I need to build some wealth for myself.*

**Deserve it:** *I am making an enormous contribution to the company. I hold down the main client and put out major fires every day. I deserve a share.*

**Pressure from others:** *The holidays are coming up and I have to face my in-laws once more, and they will spend the whole time talking about the successful guys their daughter could have married. And my brother-in-law the financial planner will be bugging me, too. They all say I deserve a slice of the pie, and, as much as I hate to say it, I agree with them.*

**Universal response:** Everything you say is true. In the best of all possible worlds, I would wave a wand and give you equity right here and now. But that just doesn't work. What does work is this company, and its growth could do big things for you. Meanwhile, I'm willing to discuss an end-of-year bonus based on profitability. And when we do distribute equity, you will be handsomely rewarded.

**Nice words:** *Those are nice words, but that's all they are. I need something more.*

**Personal commitment:** I give you my personal commitment that, as long as we are successful, you will be able to make a better career for yourself here than at some bigger place. That's what we're working toward. My goal is for both of us to be able to retire early and well.

## ADAPTATIONS

This script can be modified to:
- Turn down an employee's request to have his name on the door
- Turn down an employee's request to have his own subsidiary

## KEY POINTS

- Talk up the employee's value before he does, and take away this argument.
- If the employee says he deserves equity, agree.
- Stress the bright future for the company and the employee.
- Give the employee a strong personal commitment that he will be included in an equity redistribution, if and when one happens.

# Asking for Cooperation from a Competitor

## 34

## STRATEGY

Asking for help is seldom easy, especially for folks as independent as the self-employed. But if doing so saves you precious time, money, and effort, and allows you to turn a project around that much faster (and get paid that much quicker), isn't it worth it? The goal of this lifescript is asking a competitor for time- and money-saving help. You're not looking to farm out work to her; rather, she's privy to information or expertise you need that you could dig up on your own, but gleaning it from her will expedite things. Most self-employed entrepreneurs will help each other out, because they're savvy enough to realize that turnabout is fair play: if she helps you now, you'll do the same for her one day. But there are those who aren't willing to cooperate. Those are the nasty souls with whom this script is designed to help you deal.

## TACTICS

- **Attitude:** Don't grovel. Your competitor isn't above you just because she has the goods you need. The two of you are equals. She deserves professional respect, and so do you. Your attitude should be one of humbly requesting help without coming across as desperate or needy.
- **Preparation:** Make sure she indeed has the information that can help you out, either by doing some preliminary research or by talking with others who can verify your belief. Know down to the last detail exactly what it is you need from her. Be prepared to tell her what you need it for, as well as able to tell her when you need it by. Finally, decide whether or not you're willing to pay for the information, and if so, how much.
- **Timing:** Try calling her at the beginning of her day, before she really gets down to business. If you don't know her hours, try a midmorning phone call. Avoid calling on Mondays and Fridays if you can.
- **Behavior:** Whether this is someone for whom you have immense respect or someone whose face graces your office dartboard, you should be impeccably polite, especially since this conversation is likely to be on the telephone. Preface your request with "I'm hoping you can help me out with something." This immediately makes her more open to what you're about to say, since it's an implicit acknowledgment of her expert

# 34. Asking for Cooperation from a Competitor

**Icebreaker:** Hi, Debbie, it's Trista McCourt. I'm hoping you can help me out with something. I'm writing a report for Krashknott Airways on passenger preference when it comes to beverage, food, and in-flight films. I remembered you did an excellent comprehensive article on in-flight beverages for an aviation trade magazine last year. I was wondering if you still had your research and sources from the piece, and if so, if you could let me take a look at them? I'm under deadline, and it would save me a lot of time and effort.

**Won't cooperate:** *No offense, Trista, but that information is part of my competitive edge.*

**Response to refusal:** I understand your reluctance to share your "secret weapon." But I think if we cooperate, we can both take advantage of each other's knowledge and expertise. Besides, what goes around comes around: if the situation is ever reversed, I promise to help you.

**Jealous:** *Gee, that's interesting. I wonder if Krashknott would have hired you if they knew you didn't have all the necessary research. Maybe I should call them up and tell them they should have hired me.*

**Response to jealousy:** Krashknott hired me based on my skills and track record as a professional, not the research I have at my fingertips. Call them if you want. But if you do, you might want to think about how it affects your chances of working with them in the future. You're going to look petty, not to mention unprofessional.

**Wary:** *What do I get out of it?*

**Response to wariness:** I'll tell you what's in it for you: my promise that if the situation is ever reversed and you need my help, I'll give it. What goes around comes around, Debbie.

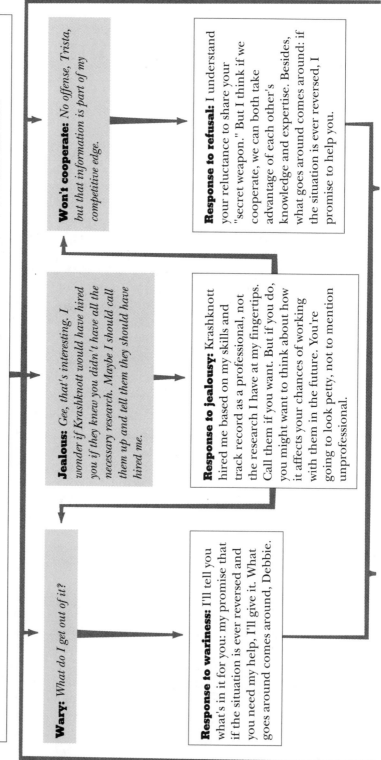

**Willing to cooperate:** *Sure, no problem—as long as I can count on you to do the same for me one day.*

**Wants compensation:** *Sure, you can have the info, but it's going to cost you. I'll give you the stuff for $500. How does that sound?*

**Willing to pay:** Look, Debbie, I've been around the block enough times to know I could hire a researcher to get this info for me to the tune of $100. That's as much as I'd be willing to spend. Take it or leave it.

**Unwilling to pay:** No offense, Debbie, but I can get this info on my own. I just thought you might be willing to help me out as a courtesy from one professional to another. But if you're not, I'll just dig it up myself.

status (even if she's not) and shows you're coming from a position of humility (even if you're not). If she's a pro, she'll be polite in return. If she's a jerk and she gives you a hard time, resist the temptation to get angry and/or hang up.

## ADAPTATIONS

This script can be modified to:

- Ask for help from a friend, family member, or coworker who you perceive feels is in some type of competition with you

## KEY POINTS

- Start your conversation with "I need your help with something."
- Make sure the person has the info you need before asking for it.
- Remember: this person is your professional equal.
- Be as specific as possible about what you need from her, as well as why.
- Let her know your deadline.
- If you can, find out what her hours are and call her early in her day. If you don't know, call her midmorning.
- Be polite and direct.
- Don't lose your temper if she acts like a jerk.

# Inviting a Competitor to Become Your Partner

## 35

## STRATEGY

There are times when it's in the best interests of both parties for competitors to become partners. Perhaps you've gotten an opportunity to take on a much larger job than you've ever tackled, or maybe you've got a chance to get into an industry you've never dealt with. Taking on a partner from the ranks of your competitors can give you both a chance to increase your bottom line and expand your horizons. Of course, not every competitor sees the pros right away. Someone might be so used to battling with you for work that he can't see beyond the competition and focus on the common good. The goal of this script is to point out the forest, not just the trees. One caveat, however: unless the individual is irreplaceable, give serious thought before twisting someone's arm to come aboard. A reluctant crew member can lead to either a mutiny or a wreck.

## TACTICS

- **Attitude:** This is a win-win situation. You have the utmost respect for your competitor/colleague and know you can both learn a great deal from each other. The opportunity is one neither of you would have alone.
- **Preparation:** Know what's involved in such a joint venture. Define what you believe the roles, responsibilities, and returns will be.
- **Timing:** As soon as you see an opportunity that you'd need a partner to pursue, make your approach. Delay changes in the terms of the arrangement. If you've already lined up a project, you'll want to take the lead and your competitor/colleague will be more of a junior partner. If the project isn't already lined up, you'll have a chance to become real partners.
- **Behavior:** Approach the discussion with enthusiasm, respect, and positive expectations. You can hold the dialogue either over the telephone or in person. If you do meet face-to-face, do so on neutral ground.

# 35. Inviting a Competitor to Become Your Partner

**Icebreaker:** Hi, Jim. I'm sure you know I've always admired your work enormously. I've just come across an exciting opportunity that requires more expertise and resources than I can manage alone. I immediately thought of you. If we combine forces we could offer the client a package that would meet his needs, and in the process we'll make some money and expand our own individual horizons.

**Agrees:** *I admire your work as well. I'm sure we can work together on a large project. Tell me more about it.*

**Interested:** *It sounds intriguing. Tell me more about the project and exactly what kind of partnership you had in mind.*

**Rejection:** *You've got to be kidding. Absolutely not. There's no way we could work together.*

**Distrusting:** *We've been competitors for our entire professional lives. Why would you think that we could suddenly work together now?*

**Let's define roles:** Terrific. I've thought a lot about what may be involved, what roles we each could play, and how we could divide the responsibilities and returns. How about meeting for lunch to discuss the project?

**Think about it:** I'm sorry you feel that way. I really do admire your work and I respect you personally. I had hoped we could work together for our mutual benefit. Please think about it overnight and call me if you change your mind. You were my first choice, so if you're truly not interested I need to begin looking for another partner. I'll call you again tomorrow.

**Share interests:** I know we've had differences in the past. But we share a commitment to excellent work and desires to grow our businesses and make as much money as we can. This project offers us opportunities for all that . . . and more. I've thought about some ways we could share the roles, responsibilities, and return and would love to get your ideas on them. How about getting together for lunch to discuss the project?

## ADAPTATIONS

This script can be modified to:
- Forge a political alliance with someone "from the other side"
- Organize two competing groups into a unified front

## KEY POINTS

- Remember that you will both benefit from a joint venture.
- State your admiration and respect for his skills and abilities.
- State that you want to share the project, but leave details for a later discussion.
- Ask to schedule the subsequent meeting at a neutral site.

# Renegotiating a Lease with Your Landlord

## 36

## STRATEGY

Asking your landlord to renegotiate your lease is certain to trigger an unhappy response. Realize your landlord is also entitled to raise your rent, so be ready to compromise. There are two possibilities here: getting a rent reduction or avoiding an increase in your current rent. Requesting that your rent remain the same is an uphill battle. Suggest renewing your lease at the current rent and then increasing the rent the following year. Explain your financial situation; business is slow, but your next fiscal year shows signs of improvement. Your landlord wants a steady paying tenant, so she may be flexible. There's no way to avoid an increase permanently, but if you delay the inevitable you've earned a victory.

An even tougher battle is asking for a rent reduction. In this case, emphasize that you'll agree to a rent increase when your business is doing better. Convince your landlord that business will improve, but you need a temporary break in the rent. Assure her you'll agree to an increase down the road and she may be receptive to your alternatives. Another compromise is offering to sign a lease that provides incremental increases. For example, if you're seeking a reduction, suggest the rent be slightly reduced this year, return to its original level the following year, and increase the third year. Your landlord must understand you'll be a long-term tenant who will pay rent increases in the future. She's likely to have counterdemands, so be open to her suggestions. If you agree to her conditions, she's more likely to agree to yours.

## TACTICS

- **Attitude:** Be humble, but not a pushover. You're in the weaker position, but that doesn't mean you have to give up. Keep probing for a mutually satisfactory compromise.
- **Timing:** Don't wait until the last minute. Negotiate well in advance of the expiration of your lease. Try to schedule a meeting right after a rent payment.
- **Preparation:** Anticipate her reaction to your alternative payment options. Formulate responses to each scenario. If you can answer her inquiries quickly and confidently, she may agree to your request.
- **Behavior:** Your landlord may be angry about your attempt to renegotiate. Don't let yourself get bogged down in anger and guilt. Keep the conversation moving in a positive direction. Continue searching for a common ground.

# 36. Renegotiating a Lease with Your Landlord

**Icebreaker:** I need to discuss the conditions of my lease with you. It's almost time for me to renew and I'm hoping you can help me and my business.

**Same rent:** I'd like to renew the lease for the same amount. As you know my business is just starting to gain momentum and a rent increase would jeopardize its success. If you would agree to holding off on a rent increase for another year it would allow my business to prosper and grow. Then, next year, I'd be happy to agree to a rent increase.

**Take it or leave it:** *Are you kidding? Hey, it's a tough world and its too bad you're having problems, but I'm planning on a 10 percent rent increase. That's the new lease offer—take it or leave it.*

**Rent reduced:** One of my clients reneged on a large payment, which has resulted in a setback to my business. I'd like to request a temporary reduction in my rent. I understand this is an unusual request, but unfortunately I find myself in a difficult situation. I've signed some new clients, but it will take a while for the business to regain momentum. After I've recouped my losses, I'd gladly agree to a rent increase.

**Pack it in:** *A reduction! Not a chance. In fact, I'm instituting a 10 percent rent increase. I don't think there's anything unfair about that. If your business isn't doing well, maybe it's time to pack it in.*

**Compromise 1:** I understand your reaction, but please hear me out. If you can leave the rent the same for this year, then I'll sign a lease raising the rent for the following year. I don't want to cheat you out of rent; I'm just asking for a chance to let my business succeed.

**Compromise 2:** I know it's a lot to ask, but I think it will pay off in the end for both of us. If you can reduce the rent this year, I'll agree to pay an increase next year. If the rent goes up now I'll have to move and it will cost you time and money to find a new tenant. By sticking with me, you'll get the guarantee of money this year and an increase the next.

**Too risky:** *How do I know you'll be successful? If your business does poorly, I'm not going to get my rent. I can't take a chance. Either pay the new rent or I won't renew your lease.*

**Outright no:** *A renewal without an increase is simply out of the question. I don't care what you tell me about next year, or the next twenty years. I'll take my chances looking for a new tenant. Promises don't mean anything and who knows what is going to happen to your business. The rent is going up.*

**Counteroffer:** *If I agree to your proposal this year, then I'll want a 15 percent increase over the next two years. If I make a concession, I think you should also.*

**Will have money:** I've signed contracts with new clients that will insure more money for my business, but I need time for the work to be completed. This is a temporary problem that I'm already beginning to solve. As soon as the new money flows in, I'll pay more rent. Until then, I'm hoping for your cooperation.

**Okay:** I'm willing to agree to an increase, but how about 12 percent? I appreciate you trying to help me solve the problem, but 15 is too high. A 12 percent increase a year from now seems reasonable.

**Final no:** *I'm sorry. There's simply no way I can work that way. If you can't pay the new rent you'll have to move.*

**Victory:** *All right, I see your point. You're in a tough spot and I'll help you now, but as soon as your business starts to pick up, I expect to renegotiate the lease and increase the rent.*

**Concede:** I'll make preparations to move. If you're not able to secure a new tenant willing to pay more rent, I hope you'll reconsider. Perhaps we can discuss it at the end of the month.

**Express thanks:** I appreciate your help and understanding. As soon as you have the lease renewal ready, I'll sign. Thanks again.

## ADAPTATIONS

This script can be modified to:
- Renegotiate a work contract in your favor
- Renegotiate the payment of an outstanding loan

## KEY POINTS

- Deflect anger and be prepared to compromise.
- Emphasize that your financial problem is temporary.
- Express a willingness to pay rent increases in the future.
- Be receptive to counteroffers from your landlord.
- Try to meet her halfway. You're more likely to reach an agreement if you both give a little ground.
- If she says no initially, suggest speaking again in a couple of weeks. If she can't find a new tenant right away, you may be able to stay.

# Asking Your Landlord for Rent Forbearance

## 37

## STRATEGY

Meet with your landlord as soon as you realize you won't be able to make your monthly rent payment. The sooner you alert your landlord to a problem, the better chance you have of negotiating an acceptable compromise. Make him understand that your inability to pay is temporary and you'll pay back the rent within a reasonable amount of time. You need solid evidence that you'll have the money in a few months. Empty excuses and promises are only going to accelerate eviction proceedings. Point to a light at the end of the tunnel, a time in the near future when you can pay the outstanding debt. If your landlord realizes you have a realistic timetable for payment, he's likely to compromise. But he also may demand a partial payment or charge late fees. Only agree to terms that are truly affordable. Your landlord will appreciate your meeting him halfway. If you're really strapped and simply have no cash, explain that you need to defer payment for a couple of months. If your landlord insists on being paid, explain that you can't give what you don't have. Emphasize that you intend to pay in full; it's just going to take a few months. He may threaten you with eviction. Don't panic; explain to him what he already knows: that eviction will take at least six months and, by following your suggestion, he'll have the money in half as much time.

## TACTICS

- **Attitude:** Be firm about not being able to pay, but receptive to reasonable compromises or alternatives. Make your landlord understand your situation and emphasize your willingness to pay in the near future.
- **Timing:** The more advance notice, the better. Discuss deferring payment as soon as you realize you won't be able to pay on time.
- **Preparation:** Read your lease to see if it covers rent forbearance. Refer to sections regarding late payments. Have in mind a timetable for payment to discuss with your landlord. Before negotiating, decide what forms of partial payment or late fees you can afford.
- **Behavior:** Keep the meeting friendly. Avoid a dialogue about who's to blame and your inability to make payments. Keep it positive and discuss when you'll be able to pay.

# 37. Asking Your Landlord for Rent Forbearance

**Icebreaker:** I need to speak with you about my rent. A customer is late with a payment (or other explanation) and that has drained my bank account. I'm in a financial bind and I won't be able to pay rent for the next two months. This is a temporary problem and I anticipate paying you back in full after a couple of months.

**Angry:** *I don't care about your business. I care about my rent check. You signed a lease agreeing to pay me. I don't hand out extensions. Pay me or I'll see you in court.*

**Upset:** *I'm sorry to hear about your problems, but I need money too. Is there any way you can take a loan or borrow money from your family?*

**Reasonable:** *I understand your position, but you have a responsibility. Is there any way you can pay some of the rent now and some later?*

**Reason with him:** I was hoping we could resolve this together. I intend to pay you in a couple of months, I'm just asking for a little extra time. Going to court will be expensive, not to mention time-consuming. If I can pay you in a couple of months, we can avoid the trouble and you'll get your rent money.

**No money:** I've explored every possible way to generate money and I'm afraid there's no alternative. I feel badly, but I'll be able to pay in a couple of months. I have customers paying bills in the next two months. After two months, I'll have enough money to repay you.

**Pay half now:** It'll be tight, but I think I can come up with half the rent for the next couple of months. As soon as business picks up, I'll be able to pay the remainder.

**Late fees:** You can defer payment, but you'll have to pay late fees. Each month you miss I'll charge you an additional 5 percent of your monthly lease. As long as you pay the late fee, you can stay.

**No go:** Other tenants have tried to run this scam on me before. You have to pay your rent in full or I'll evict you. I'm not gonna let you jerk me around for months delaying the inevitable.

**Half pay okay:** If you pay half the rent I'll allow you to delay payment, but only for a couple of months. After, say, two months, you have to pay back the outstanding amount.

**Reduce late fee:** I was hoping we could waive the late fee. I've come to you in good faith and given plenty of advance notice. However, if you need to charge a fee, would you agree to 2 percent?

**Better late than never:** I'm sorry you feel that way. If I'm evicted, I'll go out of business and you won't be able to collect any of the rent. By allowing me to defer, you get the money in a couple of months.

**Agrees:** All right, but I want you to update me on your situation each month. After two months, if you can't pay, we're going to have to talk about other solutions.

**No cash:** I'm sorry, but I don't have any money to give you. It's financially impossible for me to pay late fees or half the rent. I was hoping my honesty, good record of tenancy, and full intention of payment would count for something. In a couple of months, I'll be able to pay the outstanding amount, but due to my current situation, that's all I can offer.

**Okay:** Two percent sounds like a fair compromise. You can pay the outstanding amount, plus the late fees, in two months. I expect full payment at that time.

**Express thanks:** That sounds like a perfectly reasonable agreement. I'll be sure and keep you apprised of my financial situation. Thank you.

## ADAPTATIONS

This script can be modified to:
- Delay payment to a credit card company
- Defer payment of school tuition or loans

## KEY POINTS

- Contact your landlord as soon as you realize you won't be able to pay the rent.
- Make it clear that this is a temporary financial problem.
- Emphasize that you're going to pay the rent; you just need to defer for a couple of months.
- If financially possible, meet him halfway by agreeing to pay some of the rent or reasonable late fees.
- If he threatens eviction, explain why allowing you an extension makes more sense financially. If he evicts you, he'll never get his money.

# Renegotiating a Proposed Insurance Settlement

## 38

## STRATEGY

If you bought your insurance through a broker or agent, you should push her hard to get her to work as your advocate before you resort to this script. Remind your broker of your standing in the community and of all the people you talk to every day, and suggest that it is in her best interest to get you a better settlement. While you may have a stronger motivation, the broker will have a better shot at getting you more money since she does more business with the insurance company. Push the broker especially hard if you feel she misrepresented the nature of the coverage you needed. Be aware that in some cases the broker may tap her own Errors and Omissions insurance policy to pay the difference between what you have been offered and what you want. If the broker fails, you'll want to contact the insurance company yourself, and work your way up the ladder until you reach someone with the authority and the inclination to reconsider your settlement.

## TACTICS

- **Attitude:** Know why you think you are entitled to more money. Run your arguments past your broker, so you know where you'll find resistance. The odds are, for example, that your policy will pay for only a replacement (not an upgrade) of a piece of equipment such as a computer. In that case you will be arguing that you are entitled to more to cover the "extra expense" of installing software, or the cost of business interruption, if either of those are covered by your policy.
- **Preparation:** Have your policy number available, and the letter you received offering you a settlement. Keep track of every conversation you have so you can refer back to it.
- **Timing:** Make the first call when your broker returns empty-handed. Place your call early in the day. You may get lucky and reach an executive before her secretary is screening her calls. Barring that, realize that this is likely to be a time-consuming and frustrating process, with no guarantee of success. You will have to be persistent—you are asking people who live by the rules to make an exception.

# 38. Renegotiating a Proposed Insurance Settlement

**Icebreaker:** My name is Ms. Jacobs. I just received a letter from your company offering me a settlement of $2,000 for my stolen computer. I think there has been some kind of misunderstanding. This figure does not appropriately reflect the value of my loss. I can document that it would cost over $9,000 to replace it. If I supply the documentation, can you change the settlement to reflect the true value?

**Denial:** *I have your file on screen. You lost a 1995, 18-pound Arkansas Electronics Laptop. The amount of $2,000 is the top our chart lets us pay for one of those.*

**This is an exceptional situation:** I understand that's all the chart lists for a basic, stripped-down model. But this model had been upgraded to 300 RAM, and it was attached to a new 48-inch monitor, two CD-ROM drives, and a 56.6 modem. It had a specially designed peripheral ergonomic keyboard, as well as a leather carrying case. In addition, it was loaded with thousands of dollars' worth of software that took more than 500 hours to load. All that cost me $25,000, but I'm willing to settle for less because I understand you have to depreciate items stolen. Can we agree on $9,000? And could you give me your name please?

**Denial 2:** *I'm Ms. Lewis. I'm also sorry, but I'm only allowed to go by the chart.*

**Push the up button:** I understand. I appreciate the fact you processed my claim so quickly, but I'm sure you understand that this matter is very important to me. I'm going to have to appeal to the next level. May I have the name and phone number of your supervisor or manager?

**Boots you upstairs:** *My supervisor's name is Toni Piquet, and her extension is 666. I'd be happy to connect you.*

**Restate case:** Hello, Ms. Piquet. My name is Ms. Jacobs. I am calling you at the suggestion of Ms. Lewis in your claims department. I called her with respect to my claim, file #094780122.

**Delays:** *I'll have to review the matter with Lewis.*

**Open to possibility:** *Ms. Lewis updated me on your case, and you've made some good points. If you send the documentation to my attention, and I'll personally review the matter.*

**Push for answer:** I can call you back this afternoon or tomorrow morning to discuss this. Which would you prefer?

**Express thanks:** Thank you. I appreciate your understanding of the importance and value of technology to small-business people. I will send you the documentation and call you on Friday.

**Denial again:** *Sorry. But even with all the backup, policy requires that I go by the chart.*

**Return call:** Ms. Piquet, this is Ms. Jacobs. I spoke with you earlier this week about my claim for stolen computer equipment and then sent you the added documentation you requested. On the basis of what I sent you, can we now agree on a settlement of $9,000?

**Agrees:** *Yes, after reviewing your material I think we can agree to that.*

**Express thanks:** Thank you. I will send you a letter today confirming this conversation.

- **Behavior:** Keep going until you talk to the top person in the claims department, and the people she reports to. Eventually, you could reach someone for whom it is worth more to settle with you than to spend time talking to you. Be friendly to everyone you talk with, but move swiftly up the insurance company's ladder as soon as it becomes clear the person you're talking to can't, or won't, agree to your request. Remain sincere and genuine about your request; if you become angry, you may not even get the name of the next person to talk to.

## ADAPTATIONS

This script can be modified to:
- Appeal an unsatisfactory appraisal
- Appeal a health insurance claim denial
- Renegotiate a moving or transfer allowance

## KEY POINTS

- Start your script over with each new contact. Don't assume the information has been passed on.
- Keep working until you get a yes.
- If you have to give someone time to review, call her back. Do not wait for a call.
- Throw documentation at anyone who will accept it.
- Keep the conversation centered on the value of your loss.
- Avoid discussion about the wording of the policy. This is about your loss.
- Keep a dated log of every name, number, conversation, and result.

5/04  $1.—